D0251606

CHUCK NORRIS
LONGER AND HARDER

The Complete Chronicle of the World's
DEADLIEST, SEXIEST,
and **BEARDIEST** Man

IAN SPECTOR

GOTHAM BOOKS

Some of the material in this book was previously published in *The Truth About Chuck Norris*, *Chuck Norris vs. Mr. T*, *Chuck Norris Cannot Be Stopped*, and *The Last Stand of Chuck Norris*.

GOTHAM BOOKS
Published by Penguin Group (USA) Inc.
Penguin Group (USA) Inc., 375 Hudson Street, New York, New York 10014, USA
Penguin Group (Canada), 90 Eglinton Avenue East, Suite 700, Toronto, Ontario M4P
2Y3, Canada (a division of Pearson Penguin Canada Inc.)
Penguin Books Ltd, 80 Strand, London WC2R 0RL, England
Penguin Ireland, 25 St Stephen's Green, Dublin 2, Ireland (a division of Penguin
Books Ltd)
Penguin Group (Australia), 707 Collins Street, Melbourne, Victoria 3008, Australia
(a division of Pearson Australia Group Pty Ltd)
Penguin Books India Pvt Ltd, 11 Community Centre, Panchsheel Park, New
Delhi-110 017, India
Penguin Group (NZ), 67 Apollo Drive, Rosedale, Auckland 0632, New Zealand (a
division of Pearson New Zealand Ltd)
Penguin Books, Rosebank Office Park, 181 Jan Smuts Avenue, Parktown North 2193,
South Africa
Penguin China, B7 Jaiming Center, 27 East Third Ring Road North, Chaoyang
District, Beijing 100020, China

Penguin Books Ltd, Registered Offices: 80 Strand, London WC2R 0RL, England

Published by Gotham Books, a member of Penguin Group (USA) Inc.

First printing, November 2012
10 9 8 7 6 5 4 3 2

Copyright © 2012 by Ian Spector

Illustrations by Angelo Vildasol

All rights reserved. No part of this book may be reproduced, scanned, or
distributed in any printed or electronic form without permission. Please do not
participate in or encourage piracy of copyrighted materials in violation of the
author's rights. Purchase only authorized editions.

Gotham Books and the skyscraper logo are trademarks of Penguin Group (USA) Inc.

LIBRARY OF CONGRESS CATALOGING-IN-PUBLICATION DATA
Spector, Ian.
  Chuck Norris : longer and harder : the complete chronicle of the world's
deadliest, sexiest, and beardiest man / Ian Spector.
    p. cm.
  ISBN 978-1-592-40793-4 (pbk.)
  1. American wit and humor. 2. Norris, Chuck, 1940—Humor. I. Title.
PN6165.S6775 2012
796.8092—dc23
                              2012022600
Printed in the United States of America
Set in Rockwell
Designed by Spring Hoteling

While the author has made every effort to provide accurate telephone numbers,
Internet addresses, and other contact information at the time of publication, neither
the publisher nor the author assumes any responsibility for errors, or for changes that
occur after publication. Further, publisher does not have any control over and does
not assume any responsibility for author or third-party websites or their content.

To everyone who has always
wanted a book dedicated just to them.

GUNS DON'T KILL PEOPLE, CHUCK NORRIS DOES.

When an episode of *Walker, Texas Ranger* aired in France, the French surrendered to Chuck Norris just to be on the safe side.

Chuck Norris can eat just one Lay's potato chip.

Chuck Norris killed the pope with a roundhouse kick to the chest after an argument over who had a better beard, Jesus or Norris.

WHEN CHUCK NORRIS BLEEDS, OAK TREES SPROUT UP FROM WHERE THE BLOOD FELL.

Chuck Norris is strong enough to punch through steel, yet delicate enough to cradle a newborn to sleep.

Chuck Norris got drunk and fucked the Statue of Liberty, then bragged about it to the Lincoln Memorial.

CHUCK NORRIS CAN FIT FIVE BILLIARD BALLS IN HIS MOUTH.

Chuck Norris was born of the Greek gods Ares and Hermes in a grand session of butt sex that may never be equaled.

The only person to ever beat Chuck Norris in a game of rock-paper-scissors was a Mexican astronaut that went by the alias "Eduardo the Magnificent."

Occasionally Chuck Norris will call up the Power Rangers just to say hi.

CHUCK NORRIS EATS PENCILS AND MARKERS FOR BREAKFAST, AND SHITS OUT MASTERPIECES BY DINNER.

The Book of Revelation was actually written by Chuck Norris in a moment of prophecy.

In one episode of *The Fresh Prince of Bel-Air*, Chuck Norris replaced Carlton for a whole scene and nobody noticed.

Chuck Norris once shot a German plane down with his finger by pointing at it and yelling, **"Bang!"**

CHUCK NORRIS CAN STOP TIME FOR UP TO TWO HOURS BY THINKING ABOUT PINEAPPLES.

Chuck Norris punched a woman in the vagina when she didn't give him exact change.

Chuck Norris, when clean-shaven, radiates the heat of three suns.

CHUCK NORRIS WAS THE FIRST PERSON TO TAME A DINOSAUR.

Chuck Norris has no concept of time; if you go to his house you won't find a single clock. When you ask to leave because it's getting late he stares at you blankly until you sit back down.

CHUCK NORRIS ONCE TOLD HIS MUSTACHE TO STRANGLE AN ENTIRE VIETNAMESE VILLAGE.

Chuck Norris had no costars on the set of *Walker, Texas Ranger*. He played every role, even the hot chick.

Chuck Norris actually picks his watches based on how many atmospheres they can withstand.

Every piece of furniture in Chuck Norris's house is a Total Gym.

Chuck Norris has a $17 million life insurance policy out on his shadow.

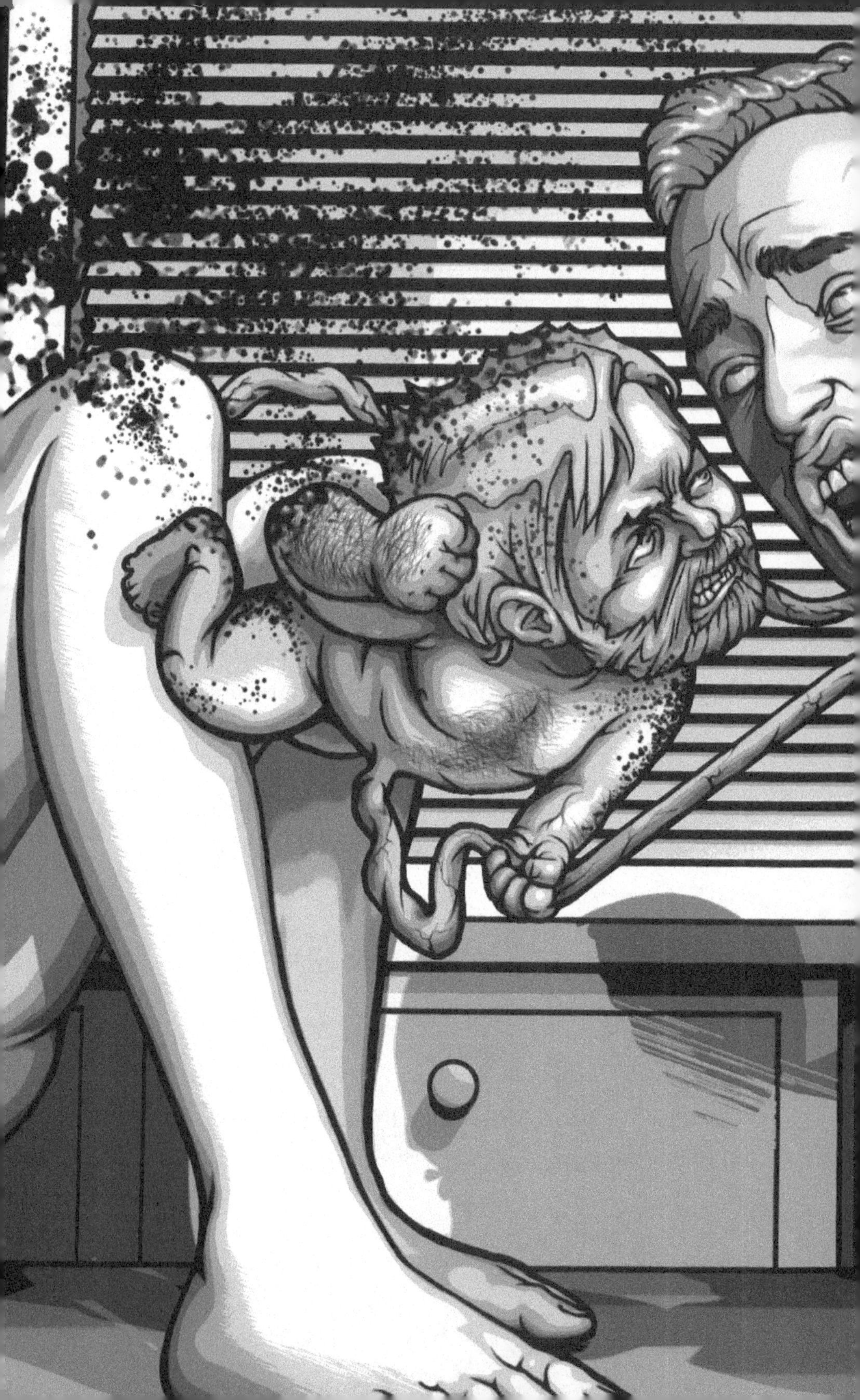

RATHER THAN BEING BIRTHED LIKE
A NORMAL CHILD, CHUCK NORRIS
INSTEAD DECIDED TO PUNCH HIS
WAY OUT OF HIS MOTHER'S WOMB.
HENCE THE TERM "C-SECTION."

CHUCK NORRIS IS THE REASON THAT JACK IS IN A BOX.

If you can see Chuck Norris, he can see you. If you can't see Chuck Norris, you may be only seconds away from death.

There are a combined thirty-nine miles of bridges, tunnels, and highways in the world named after Chuck Norris but only six of them are public roads outside his fort.

CHUCK NORRIS'S BODY HAIR IS TEN TIMES STRONGER THAN SPIDER SILK AND FIFTY TIMES STICKIER.

If you've ever met a woman with crooked teeth, you've met a woman who has given Chuck Norris a blow job.

Chuck Norris once boned the Mona Lisa, which is why she smiles.

CHUCK NORRIS ROUTINELY CRUSHES CANS ON HIS FOREHEAD. *GARBAGE CANS.*

Contrary to popular belief, Chuck Norris was dropped at Hiroshima and Nagasaki.

WHEN CHUCK NORRIS BREAKS THE LAW, THE LAW DOESN'T HEAL.

When working with Chuck Norris, common occupational hazards include crippling joint pain and death.

CHUCK NORRIS CAN MAKE
A WOMAN CLIMAX BY SIMPLY
POINTING AT HER AND SAYING,
"BOOYA."

Chuck Norris was once accused of heresy by the pope, but as it turns out, Chuck Norris is, in fact, the true son of God.

Chuck Norris doesn't lose weight; he discards it intentionally.

CHUCK NORRIS WAS NAMED AFTER HIMSELF.

CHUCK NORRIS IS THE WORLD'S BEST ACTOR BECAUSE HIS MUSTACHE IS THE WORLD'S BEST ACTING COACH.

In Indochina, Chuck Norris's left testicle is worshiped as the god of love, whereas his right testicle is viewed as a fire-breathing demon from hell.

Chuck Norris's heart beats once every week.

BIGFOOT OWNS A GRAINY VIDEO OF CHUCK NORRIS.

If Chuck Norris had a dollar and you had a dollar, Chuck would kick your ass and take your dollar.

NOCTURNAL ANIMALS JUST CAN'T SLEEP KNOWING CHUCK NORRIS LURKS ABOUT.

To prove it isn't that big of a deal to beat cancer, Chuck Norris smoked fifteen cartons of cigarettes a day for two years and acquired seven different kinds of cancer only to rid them from his body by flexing for thirty minutes. Beat that, Lance Armstrong.

Chuck Norris's tears cure cancer.
Too bad he has never cried.

When playing poker with Chuck Norris, you might have the better hand, but he always has the better fist.

CHUCK NORRIS
WOULD HIT THAT.

Chuck Norris will never fully be male nor female. Doctors once asked him which he preferred. He gave them an ad for a Total Gym.

Chuck Norris can destroy ten thousand acres of rain forest with a single sneeze.

Chuck Norris's appliances don't need power buttons— just somewhere he can insert his penis.

The light at the end of the tunnel is Chuck Norris's fist rushing toward you.

IF CHUCK NORRIS HAD A DIME FOR EVERY MAN THAT DIDN'T DIE FROM HIS ROUNDHOUSE KICK, HE WOULD HAVE NO DIMES.

Chuck Norris once broke a mirror on a black cat under a ladder on Friday the thirteenth and then won the lottery.

CHUCK NORRIS JUST PISSED YOUR PANTS.

Chuck Norris keeps a horde of trained bees under his beard to let loose at a moment's notice.

In a fight between
Batman and Darth Vader,
the winner would be
CHUCK NORRIS.

CHUCK NORRIS TWEAKED HIS HARLEY TO GIVE IT FOUR-WHEEL DRIVE.

Chuck Norris invented babies because he got tired of eating the same old thing.

Chuck Norris doesn't use toothpicks; he punches himself in the teeth until the chunks of food run for their lives.

ROGER EBERT HAS RECURRING NIGHTMARES ABOUT THE DAY CHUCK NORRIS AND TYLER PERRY WORK ON A MOVIE TOGETHER.

Chuck Norris began the Church of England in 1799, back when his nickname was "England."

Objects in Chuck Norris's side view mirrors are closer to death than they appear.

THE CHIEF EXPORT OF CHUCK NORRIS IS PAIN.

Chuck Norris is considered a prime number in certain schools in Ontario.

CHUCK NORRIS LIVES BY ONLY ONE RULE: NO ASIAN CHICKS.

Chuck Norris was born with cowboy boots on. The spurs on his boots made sure that he wouldn't have a younger brother to compete with.

When Chuck Norris was denied a McGriddle at McDonald's because it was 10:35, he roundhouse kicked the store so hard it became a Wendy's.

DR PEPPER IS CHUCK NORRIS'S PERSONAL PHYSICIAN.

Chuck Norris once hit a deer with his car. He then put the car back on the ground and continued driving.

CHUCK NORRIS NEVER HIDES, HE ONLY SEEKS.

Chuck Norris was banned from the Olympics after he won every gold medal and melted them down to make what he called "the perfect condom."

CHUCK NORRIS IS SO SMART, STEPHEN HAWKING STOOD UP TO BOW DOWN TO HIM.

Ever see the Grand Canyon? Chuck Norris had nothing to do with it, he just went there once on a family vacation.

CHUCK NORRIS IS THE ONLY PERSON EVER CAPABLE OF TELLING IF AN AIRCRAFT LANDED IN SOIL BY TASTING IT.

Chuck Norris is not a man; he is the culmination of hundreds of years of black oppression.

CHUCK NORRIS MAKES PLANS TO BREAK PLANS.

Chuck Norris's penis is so large that it actually warps the fabric of space-time. Indeed, some researchers now theorize that the passage of time is merely a by-product of Norris's colossal erections. This is known as the "Chuck Norris's Big Cock Theory of Space-Time" and is steadily gaining acceptance among physicists.

CHUCK NORRIS HAS AN ENTIRE BLUE WHALE MOUNTED ABOVE HIS FIREPLACE.

The National Funeral Directors Association voted to make Chuck Norris their honorary president after he personally increased their business by 300 percent.

THE GREATEST TRICK THE DEVIL EVER PULLED WAS CONVINCING THE WORLD THAT CHUCK NORRIS WAS JUST AN ACTOR.

Every fourteen years Chuck Norris enters into a cocoon, emerges as Mothra, and terrorizes Tokyo.

CHUCK NORRIS IS, THEREFORE I AM AFRAID.

Chuck Norris invented the measurement the "yard," as it was much easier to say than, "Hi, my name is Chuck Norris and my dick is three feet long."

CHUCK NORRIS CAN MAKE THE KESSEL RUN IN LESS THAN TEN PARSECS.

For Texas-issued driver's licenses, there are three choices under the "Do you choose to be an organ donor?" category: "Yes," "No," or "I am Chuck Norris and I will be providing the medical community with thousands of organ donors."

Jesus follows Chuck Norris on Twitter.

CHUCK NORRIS BLOWS HIS NOSE ON SUPERMAN'S CAPE.

In China there is an ancient legend that one day a child will be born from a dragon and vanquish evil from the land. That man is not Chuck Norris, but Chuck Norris did kill that man.

Patriotic Americans know to salute Chuck Norris's dick because he has a full-size American flag flying from it.

CHUCK NORRIS ONCE INHALED A SEAGULL.

Chuck Norris's dick is so big, it has its own dick. And Chuck Norris's dick's dick is bigger than your dick.

Chuck Norris plays Ping-Pong with an ironing board and a watermelon.

CHUCK NORRIS WHISTLES IN GERMAN.

The Great Wall of China was modeled after Chuck Norris's pectoral muscles. This explains the large number of dead Asians buried within the wall.

The "clang" from *Law & Order* sounds when you ring Chuck Norris's doorbell.

CHUCK NORRIS'S ADVICE?
GROW A BEARD.

Chuck Norris once ejaculated solid gold into a river in India, bringing profit to the local villagers and causing him to be worshiped as a god.

Chuck Norris fought and won a battle at the Red Sea, which was originally called the Blue Sea.

Chuck Norris was voted "Most likely to rescue a POW using a mule kick" by his senior class.

CHUCK NORRIS DOESN'T BELIEVE IN GERMANY.

THE LIBERTY BELL WAS SCULPTED OUT OF ONE OF CHUCK NORRIS'S KIDNEY STONES.

CHUCK NORRIS DEFEATED AN ENTIRE BASEMENT OF KOREAN TEENAGERS IN *STARCRAFT*.

As well as being an actor, martial artist, and poet, Chuck Norris is also a world-renowned physicist. It was in this capacity that he once had a disagreement about steady-state theory with Stephen Hawking. Hence the wheelchair.

CHUCK NORRIS PLAYS MINESWEEPER WITH REAL MINES AND HEARTS WITH REAL HEARTS.

At Chuck Norris's bachelor party, he ate the entire cake before his friends could tell him there was a stripper in it.

**The real reason Hitler killed
himself was because he found out
Chuck Norris was Jewish.**

When Chuck Norris's wife burned the turkey one Thanksgiving, Chuck said, "Don't worry about it, honey," and went into his backyard. He came back five minutes later with a live turkey, ate it whole, and, when he threw it up a few seconds later, it was fully cooked and came with cranberry sauce. When his wife asked him how he had done it, he gave her a roundhouse kick to the face and said, "Never question Chuck Norris."

Chuck Norris can rub his stomach, pat his head, and perform an oil change at the same time.

Chuck Norris bemoans the fact that the typical American is unaware that *Walker, Texas Ranger* is an unscripted reality show.

CHUCK NORRIS MAKES HIS INTERNAL ORGANS PAY RENT.

CHUCK NORRIS IS THE ONLY 100 PERCENT EFFECTIVE FORM OF CONTRACEPTION.

FOR CHUCK NORRIS, PIMPING IS EASY.

Chuck Norris would use guns if they didn't kill people so slowly.

King Kong built the wall around Skull Island to protect himself from Chuck Norris.

CHUCK NORRIS HAS A WRANGLER BELT IN KARATE.

IN 2010, CHUCK NORRIS LAUNCHED HIS OWN FRAGRANCE, DOJO MOJO, WHICH SMELLS OF **DENIM** AND **JUSTICE**.

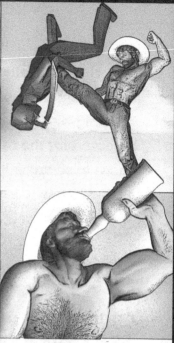

While not officially a diplomat, Chuck Norris has his own seat at the United Nations. He walked into the building by accident in 1992 and sat down in a seat reserved for the representative from Denmark, who chose to sit cross-legged on the floor rather than risk asking him to leave.

CHUCK NORRIS WAS KICKED OUT OF THE ARMY FOR NEVER CARRYING A WEAPON INTO BATTLE.

Chuck Norris's dick trains world champion cock fighters.

CHUCK NORRIS MAKES ONIONS CRY.

Chuck Norris can impregnate women with only a glance. He can also do this to men.

WHEN GOD NEEDS TO FLOSS, HE USES ONE OF CHUCK NORRIS'S BEARD HAIRS.

Chuck Norris is Tiger Woods's third, eighth, and sixteenth mistresses.

THE DOORS IN CHUCK NORRIS'S HOUSE WILL OPEN ONLY IF YOU KICK THEM DOWN.

Not only can Chuck Norris throw his voice, he is lethal with it for up to two hundred yards.

The real secret to the success of *Girls Gone Wild* is that **CHUCK NORRIS IS THE CAMERAMAN**.

Instead of warming up before a workout, Chuck Norris hammers himself to a crucifix and then pulls the stakes out with his teeth.

CHUCK NORRIS EATS COAL AND SHITS DIAMONDS.

Chuck Norris plans to rid the world of hunger by killing the hungry.

A barista in a coffee shop once called a Freedom Press a French Press in Chuck Norris's presence. There were no survivors.

Instead of having a cigarette after sex, Chuck Norris heads outside and brands his cattle.

CHUCK NORRIS IS THE BEST THING BEFORE, AFTER, AND DURING SLICED BREAD.

During a game of golf, Chuck Norris shot two holes in one, struck out nine batters, caught a three-hundred-yard pass, recorded a hat trick, and broke the single lap speed record at Daytona Speedway.

Chuck Norris's poop is used as currency in Argentina.

CHUCK NORRIS EMPLOYS A STUNT DOUBLE FOR HIS CRYING SCENES.

**When ghosts go camping,
they sit around the fire and
tell stories about Chuck Norris.**

Iceland's power is sourced completely by geothermal energy. Of course, all geothermal energy originates with Chuck Norris working out on his Total Gym inside the Earth's core.

When Chuck Norris punches you in the uterus, you become pregnant. Don't try an abortion, either; it only makes the fetus stronger.

CHUCK NORRIS WEARS A LIVE RATTLESNAKE AS A CONDOM.

Chuck Norris was the fourth wise man. He brought baby Jesus the gift of "beard." Jesus wore it proudly to his dying day. The other wise men, jealous of Chuck, used their combined influence to have him omitted from the Bible. Shortly thereafter, all three died roundhouse kick–related deaths.

The video game *Katamari Damacy* was inspired by Chuck Norris's tendency to roll Japanese families into balls and hurl them into space.

CHUCK NORRIS SMOKES ONLY THE FINEST CUBAN CIGAR ROLLERS.

Octomom got pregnant eight times over simply by watching Chuck Norris work out in an infomercial for the Total Gym.

Chuck Norris caddied for the Dalai Lama once. Instead of giving him money, the Lama offered Chuck the ability to receive total consciousness on his deathbed. Clearly upset by this offer, Chuck roundhouse kicked him into a ten-thousand-foot crevasse.

CHUCK NORRIS DOESN'T NEED TICKETS TO THE GUN SHOW BECAUSE HE IS THE MAIN EVENT.

Chuck Norris once roundhouse kicked someone so fast that they actually grew younger.

IT NEVER RAINS ON CHUCK NORRIS.

Chuck Norris was the inspiration for *Donkey Kong*, HDTV, and waterslides. Yes, waterslides.

Chuck Norris plans to assassinate four other civil rights leaders just to get an entire week off in January.

Drug lord Pablo Escobar committed suicide after viewing a VHS tape of *Delta Force 2: The Colombian Connection*.

Chuck Norris is in a rock band with the Hope Diamond, the moon, and the Aggro Crag on bass.

CHUCK NORRIS CAN BUILD A SNOWMAN OUT OF RAIN.

Someone once asked Chuck Norris if he would Like their post on Facebook. He stared at them until they burst into flames.

CHUCK NORRIS CAN DROWN A FISH.

CHUCK NORRIS ONCE ATE THREE
SEVENTY-TWO-OUNCE STEAKS IN
ONE HOUR. HE SPENT THE FIRST
FORTY-FIVE MINUTES OF THAT HOUR
HAVING SEX WITH HIS WAITRESS.

A man once broke every bone in his body to avoid
Chuck Norris doing it for him.

In the eighties, Chuck Norris marketed a children's
cereal called "Chux." It did not sell very well because
it was made entirely from **HUMAN TEETH**.

**CHUCK NORRIS ONCE MADE LOVE
TO A GRIZZLY BEAR FOR FOUR HOURS.**

**CHUCK NORRIS TRIMS HIS BEARD
WITH A DULL BAYONET.**

They use Chuck Norris's foreskin as a tarp when it
rains at Yankee Stadium.

CHUCK NORRIS'S PICKUP DOES THIRTY MILES PER GALLON OF BLOOD.

Chuck Norris is the only celebrity to have a death row named after him.

IF YOU HOLD CHUCK NORRIS'S COWBOY BOOT TO YOUR EAR, YOU CAN HEAR THE RIFF FROM "ROCK YOU LIKE A HURRICANE."

If someone asks Chuck Norris what his favorite song is, he roundhouse kicks them in the face until they beg for mercy. He then tells them that's music to his ears.

JAWBREAKERS WERE ORIGINALLY IN THE SHAPE OF CHUCK NORRIS'S FIST.

CHUCK NORRIS'S PREFERRED GOLF CART IS A MONSTER TRUCK CALLED THE VIOLATOR.

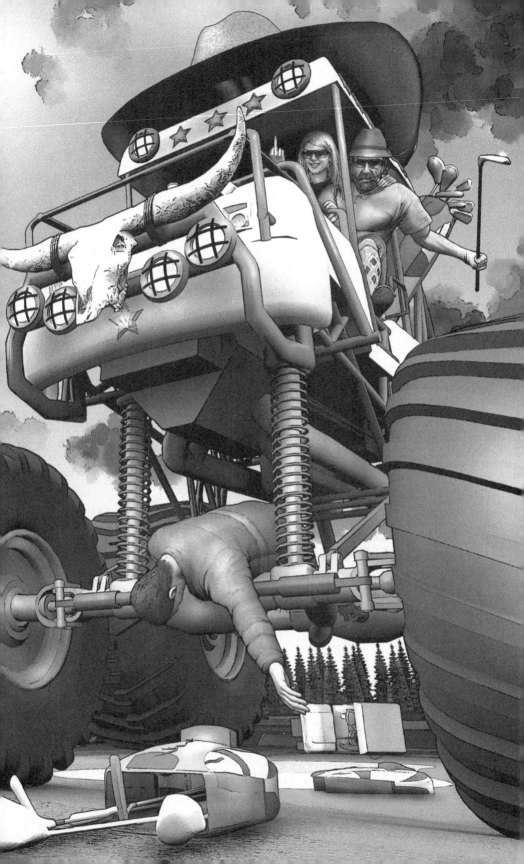

THE 2011 TEA PARTY CONVENTION WAS HELD ENTIRELY WITHIN CHUCK NORRIS'S BEARD.

Chuck Norris never has to pay a prostitute for sex, partly because they are so excited that they refuse to charge him, but mostly because he kills them.

When they say, "it's raining cats and dogs," Chuck Norris is probably just visiting the local animal hospital.

CHUCK NORRIS WASN'T BORN. HE WAS FORGED.

The last time Chuck Norris played golf on an eighteen-hole course, he shot a fourteen. This beat his previous best by two strokes.

Chuck Norris can eat a Rubik's Cube and poop it out solved.

Chuck Norris invented ice skates after he realized not everyone is born with blades attached to their feet.

CHUCK NORRIS CAN DO PUSH-UPS WITH BOTH ARMS TIED BEHIND HIS BACK.

CHUCK NORRIS'S BLOOD PRESSURE IS MEASURED IN VOLTS PER KILOGRAM.

Chuck Norris coined the phrase, "Don't come near me, motherfucker, or I'll roundhouse kick the shit out of you." The phrase has since been changed to, "Don't mess with Texas."

When Arnold says the line "I'll be back" in the first *Terminator* movie, it is implied that is he going to ask Chuck Norris for help.

CHUCK NORRIS DID NOT HAVE CHILDHOOD HEROES, ONLY COMPETITION.

CHUCK NORRIS PUTS THE "FUN" IN "FUNERAL."

Before you die, you see the ring on Chuck Norris's right hand.

ALL of Chuck Norris's teeth are wisdom teeth.

CHUCK NORRIS MOVED YOUR CHEESE.

In 1985 Chuck Norris entered a science fair for disadvantaged youths. His submission was based on the premise that the speed and force of his roundhouse kicks actually disprove many of the laws of physics. Despite lacking any actual proof for this theory, Chuck was awarded first place in all categories and a special merit award for "Please don't hurt us."

Contrary to popular belief, Chuck Norris has in fact had a sex change operation: male to Chuck Norris.

World records are just things that Chuck Norris has not yet attempted.

Rainbows are what happens when Chuck Norris roundhouse kicks Richard Simmons.

CHUCK NORRIS ONCE DROWNED A WOMAN IN A WATERBED.

To Chuck Norris, a "balanced breakfast" must include an entire seesaw covered in thumbtacks.

MacGyver used a paper clip, balloon, and pencil to make a building explode. Chuck Norris used his feet.

CHUCK NORRIS KNOWS MORE THAN TEN THOUSAND WAYS TO MOLEST A PANDA.

Billy Mays was accidentally killed during a late-night bender by Chuck Norris's beard and Keith Hernandez's mustache.

Chuck Norris once won the Kentucky Derby
RIDING A HUNGRY LION.

Chuck Norris was the original model for Brawny paper towels. He gained this position by winning a competition to see who could best intimidate a woman into a life of cleaning and servitude.

If Chuck Norris were a *Star Trek* character, he would be the ship.

KEANU REEVES STUDIED ACTING UNDER CHUCK NORRIS.

Chuck Norris can drink Bud Light and piss out Dogfish Head 90 Minute IPA.

CHUCK NORRIS'S PENIS HAS A TOENAIL.

CHUCK NORRIS FIGHTS STAINS WITH THE POWER OF TIDE.

Chuck Norris's girlfriend once asked him how much wood a woodchuck could chuck if a woodchuck could chuck wood. Chuck then shouted, *"How dare you rhyme in the presence of Chuck Norris!"* and ripped out her throat. Holding his girlfriend's bloody throat in his hand, he bellowed, *"Don't fuck with Chuck!"* Two years and five months later he realized the irony of this statement and laughed so hard that anyone within a hundred-mile radius of the blast went deaf.

Chuck Norris came up with the idea for the Total Gym after trying to bench press his own penis. He found that he needed to start with a lighter weight and work his way up.

Chuck Norris defeated Hulk Hogan at the Battle of Little Bighorn.

TIM TEBOW TEBOWS OUT OF RESPECT FOR HIS LORD AND SAVIOR, CHUCK NORRIS.

Chuck Norris can make your nose bleed with his mind.

Chuck Norris fucked your wife while you were out of town on a business trip. **TOUGH SHIT.**

Chuck Norris sold his soul to the devil for his rugged good looks and unparalleled martial arts ability. Shortly after the transaction was finalized, Chuck roundhouse kicked the devil in the face and took his soul back. The devil, who appreciates irony, couldn't stay mad and admitted he should have seen it coming. They now play poker every second Wednesday of the month.

In the late eighties, Chuck Norris once roundhouse kicked Michael Jackson so hard, he knocked all the black off him.

CHUCK NORRIS ISN'T GOD, BUT HE BEATS HIM IN GOLF.

Chuck Norris invented the hammer when he was tired of using his forehead to slam nails into wood.

Kill one man and you are a murderer; kill millions and you are a conqueror; kill them all and you are Chuck Norris.

It is commonly known that Eve was created from the rib of Adam, but few know that Chuck Norris was actually created using Adam's genitals.

CHUCK NORRIS CAN DO A WHEELIE ON A UNICYCLE.

Chuck Norris's belly button is an "innie." Inside Chuck's belly button is an alternate universe where thousands of tiny Chuck Norrises are training to get their buddies out of a Vietcong POW camp.

CHUCK NORRIS STRUCK GOLD WHILE PICKING HIS NOSE.

Chuck Norris hates serving on jury duty because his balls always set off the courthouse metal detector.

Justin Timberlake is bringing sexy back because he borrowed it from Chuck Norris.

CHUCK NORRIS IS CURRENTLY SUING NBC, CLAIMING *LAW & ORDER* ARE TRADEMARKED NAMES FOR HIS LEFT AND RIGHT LEGS.

CHUCK NORRIS WAS THE ONLY PERSON ON SEAL TEAM SIX.

Chuck Norris once donated ten liters of his own blood. After that he won the Tour de France on a pogo stick.

Some people eat pepperoni on their pizza. Some people have mushrooms. Chuck Norris usually has Venezuela.

BEFORE LEO TOLSTOY MET CHUCK NORRIS, HIS BOOK WAS CALLED *PEACE*.

It takes fourteen puppeteers to make Chuck Norris smile, but only two to make him destroy an orphanage.

While Chuck Norris was on holiday in Spain, he ate some bad paella, causing him to take the largest shit known to man. That shit is now France.

All of Chuck Norris's toes are big toes.

Chuck Norris has his own private fishing hole, which he protects at all costs; we call this spot the Bermuda Triangle.

When Chuck Norris puts his ear to a seashell, he always hears Mozart's Piano Concerto no. 27 in B Flat Major.

WHEN CHUCK NORRIS FARTS, IT SMELLS LIKE FRESHLY BAKED CINNAMON ROLLS.

**Superman owns a pair
of Chuck Norris pajamas.**

Chuck Norris currently owns the single largest collection of mummified cats in the world. When questioned about the motivation for such a collection, his only reply was, "They aren't ripe yet."

DOCTORS ONCE FOUND SIXTY DOLLARS' WORTH OF NICKELS IN CHUCK NORRIS'S STOMACH.

Contrary to popular belief, Chuck Norris did not learn martial arts. He merely rediscovered the ancient, forgotten art of Chuck Norris.

EVERY CELL IN CHUCK NORRIS'S BODY HAS ITS OWN BEARD.

Chuck Norris has a hand-tooled leather vest made from the hide of a studio executive who displeased him.

CHUCK NORRIS COVERS HIS SLIP 'N SLIDE WITH GRAVEL.

When Chuck Norris orders a Bloody Mary, he expects to be given a woman named Mary, who he then beats to a bloody pulp.

Chuck Norris once stayed up all night playing poker with tarot cards. He got a full house and eight people died.

CHUCK NORRIS IS SO FAST, HE CAN RUN AROUND THE WORLD AND PUNCH HIMSELF IN THE BACK OF THE HEAD.

CHUCK NORRIS IS THE OFFICIAL AIRLINE OF THE CINCINNATI REDS.

If you drop a phonograph needle on Chuck Norris's nipple, it plays The Beach Boys' *Pet Sounds*.

CHUCK NORRIS HAS ALL OF YOUR LOST PENS.

Chuck Norris wrote a negative review of a restaurant and the next day outraged citizens burned their entire city to the ground in shame.

Chuck Norris can lift a mountain over his head with one arm and make a perfect pitcher of Kool-Aid with the other.

If you visit Chuck Norris's house, you can buy a shirt that says, "I fellated Chuck Norris and all I got was this lousy shirt and a mouth full of radioactive semen."

ALL THE YES ALBUM COVERS ARE NORRIS FAMILY PHOTOS.

Everything Chuck Norris knows about kangaroos is false.

CHUCK NORRIS CAN CHARGE A CELL PHONE JUST BY RUBBING IT AGAINST HIS BEARD.

The phrase "rule of thumb" is derived from an old English law that stated that Chuck Norris couldn't beat your wife with anything smaller than his thumb.

Chuck Norris once wrestled a bear, an alligator, and a mountain lion all at once. He won by tying them together with an anaconda.

Chuck Norris eats his birthday cake
WITHOUT BLOWING OUT THE CANDLES.

A recent poll discovered 93 percent of women
think about Chuck Norris during sex. A related poll
discovered Chuck Norris thinks about Chuck Norris
100 percent of the time during sex.

CHUCK NORRIS REFERS TO HIMSELF IN THE FOURTH PERSON.

To keep his mind sharp, Chuck Norris plays tic-tac-toe
versus himself. He wins every time.

Every 911 call that Chuck Norris makes always begins
the same way: "Yeah, it's me again."

NEW SOUTH WALES IN AUSTRALIA WAS DEDICATED JUST ONE WEEK AFTER CHUCK NORRIS HARPOONED EVERYONE IN SOUTHERN WALES.

Jesus turned water into wine. Chuck Norris turned wine into a bad temper and an aggravated assault.

CHUCK NORRIS ONCE LEANED AGAINST A TOWER IN PISA, ITALY.

Chuck Norris is the luckiest man in the world in that he is the only person on Earth who doesn't have to worry about pissing off Chuck Norris.

Chuck Norris once had a cobra that he named Beverly. He taught it how to fetch and dial a phone. But then one day, it bit the maid. So with tears in his eyes, Chuck had to shoot the maid.

TO SAVE ON WEIGHT, CHUCK NORRIS NOW HAS NERVES OF TITANIUM.

There are three ways to do things: the right way, the wrong way, and the Chuck Norris way. The Chuck Norris way is the same as the wrong way, but with more roundhouse kicks.

CHUCK NORRIS CAN TRAVEL THROUGH TIME BY RUNNING AT EIGHTY-EIGHT MILES PER HOUR.

Chuck Norris's family crest depicts a barracuda eating Neil Armstrong.

CHUCK NORRIS HAS THE DIRECTIONS TO SESAME STREET IN HIS GPS BUT REFUSES TO TELL ANYONE.

When Alexander Graham Bell made the first phone call, all he heard on the other end was Chuck Norris's heavy breathing.

Chuck Norris is the only survivor of the *HINDENBURG*, the *TITANIC*, and **NEW COKE**.

CHUCK NORRIS WAS THE ORIGINAL DANNY TANNER ON THE HIT FAMILY SITCOM *FULL HOUSE.* HE WAS REPLACED BY BOB SAGET AFTER AN UNFORTUNATE INCIDENT WITH ONE OF THE OLSEN TRIPLETS.

Chuck Norris once roundhouse kicked someone so hard that his foot broke the speed of light, went back in time, and killed Amelia Earhart while she was flying over the Pacific Ocean.

CHUCK NORRIS HAS NEVER BEEN TO ALBANIA, BUT HE HAS HAD SEX WITH MORE ALBANIANS THAN MOST ALBANIANS.

MOST PEOPLE FEAR THE REAPER. CHUCK NORRIS CONSIDERS HIM "A PROMISING ROOKIE."

Chuck Norris is actually an extremely talented harpsichordist who has brought audiences to tears with his rendition of "Thong Song."

Chuck Norris killed Saddam Hussein not because Saddam was building weapons of mass destruction, but because Saddam's mustache insulted Chuck Norris's beard.

ALL FACTS ARE IN SOME WAY ABOUT CHUCK NORRIS.

Chuck Norris will only charter a helicopter if it can take off in slow motion with no fewer than six hundred pounds of explosives detonating behind it.

CHUCK NORRIS CAN TURN A WALRUS INSIDE OUT WITH HIS BARE HANDS.

The only reason we live in a world without *Back to the Future Part IV* is because Chuck Norris went back in time and roundhouse kicked Michael J. Fox so hard that he ended up with Parkinson's, thereby preventing the film from ever being made.

CHUCK NORRIS RUNS WINDOWS 8 ON HIS ETCH A SKETCH.

For an extra kick, Chuck Norris spikes his aftershave with just a splash of battery acid.

Chuck Norris's lungs are made from burlap sacks full of Beefaroni.

During the Great Rocky Mountain Blackout of 2004, the city of Las Vegas was powered for two days entirely by friction generated on Chuck Norris's beard.

CHUCK NORRIS CAN HIT A GRAND SLAM WITH THE BASES EMPTY.

CHUCK NORRIS'S
BLOOD TYPE IS D.O.A.

Chuck Norris once broke into a sealed, six-inch-thick lead vault using nothing but a paper clip, a wad of chewing gum, MacGyver's rib cage, and the combination.

WHEN CHUCK NORRIS PLAYED FOR THE DODGERS, HE WORE NUMBER FORTY-TWO AND NOBODY SAID A WORD.

Chuck Norris's favorite boot has been up so many asses, it received a lifetime achievement award from the American Society of Proctologists.

BEFORE A DODO SHIT ON CHUCK NORRIS'S PICKUP TRUCK, THE DODO WAS THE MOST COMMON SPECIES OF BIRD IN THE WORLD.

The only reason it was not called *The CBS Evening News with Chuck Norris* is that Dan Rather once pulled a thorn out of Chuck's paw.

Chuck Norris once destroyed over one thousand panes of glass in the NorthPark Center mall in Dallas, Texas, merely by window-shopping.

CHUCK NORRIS CAN COMMIT A FATAL HIT-AND-RUN ON FOOT.

Chuck Norris sent one of his children to Guantanamo for three months for not taking out the trash.

CHUCK NORRIS IS THE PATRON SAINT OF PATRON SAINTS.

Doctors debate the nutritional benefits of the Chuck Norris Salad because it contains ten pounds of raw beef, one head of lettuce, and two heads of state.

WHEN THE INCREDIBLE HULK GETS ANGRY HE TURNS INTO CHUCK NORRIS.

Noah was the only man notified before Chuck Norris relieved himself in the Atlantic Ocean.

Whenever Chuck Norris is witnessed committing a crime, the police take the description as "a twentysomething black male."

China used to border the United States until Chuck Norris roundhouse kicked it all the way through the earth and out the other side.

CHUCK NORRIS HAS THREE BIRTHDAYS A YEAR.

Tom Clancy has to pay royalties to Chuck Norris because *The Sum of All Fears* was originally the title of Chuck's autobiography.

At a 1985 rape trial, when questioned by the prosecutor whether he'd forced a woman to have sex with him, Chuck Norris replied, "I didn't force her. I Delta Forced her." Chuck Norris was acquitted of all charges.

Chuck Norris doesn't have normal white blood cells like you and me. His have a small black ring around them. This signifies that they are black belts and they roundhouse kick the shit out of viruses. That's why Chuck Norris never gets ill.

CHUCK NORRIS IS WHERE BABIES COME FROM.

When Chuck Norris plays Super Mario Bros., the princess is always in the first castle.

CHUCK NORRIS OPERATES THE LARGEST FIRE-BREATHING DRAGON FARM.

Chuck Norris has had sex in every U.S. embassy in the Northern Hemisphere.

CHUCK NORRIS ISN'T REALLY A CAT PERSON, WHICH IS WHY HE ONLY HAS ONE LION.

THE SPURS ON CHUCK NORRIS'S BOOTS HAVE A THREE-TON TOWING CAPACITY.

Chuck Norris made killing cool. Before everybody was like, "Killing? Yeah, right!" But now everybody is like, "Sweet."

Mike Tyson has a standing invitation to any of Chuck Norris's renowned banquets made entirely from human ears.

Chuck Norris's orthodox boxing stance has been certified kosher by the Central Rabbinical Congress of the United States and Canada.

The 1977 film *Breaker! Breaker!* stars Chuck Norris as a truck driver who literally destroys an entire town using only eighteen-wheelers.

CHUCK NORRIS IS THE REASON WHY BAD THINGS HAPPEN TO GOOD PEOPLE.

By presidential decree, every time Chuck Norris trims his beard, the whiskers are gathered and buried at Arlington National Cemetery with full honors.

Chuck Norris knows we put a man on the moon because Chuck Norris was the one who threw him there.

WHEN HE IS ALONE AT NIGHT, CHUCK NORRIS LIKES TO WEAR SLIPPERS WITH BUNNIES ON THEM. REAL LIVE BUNNIES.

People who are antiunion are just afraid of the thought of Chuck Norris striking anything.

WHEN CHUCK NORRIS GOES ON A VEGAN DIET, HE ONLY EATS VEGANS.

Chuck Norris's social security is knowing that society will continue to exist so long as he's around.

Chuck Norris once fell out of a fourteen-story window into love.

CHUCK NORRIS ONLY WEARS SUITS MADE FROM THE FINEST ITALIAN MARBLE.

Chuck Norris can make origami with his foldout couch.

Chuck Norris owns the greatest poker face of all time. It helped him win the 1983 World Series of Poker despite his holding just a joker, a Get Out of Jail Free Monopoly card, a 2 of clubs, a 7 of spades, and a green number 4 card from the game Uno.

CHUCK NORRIS PERFORMS BACK-ALLEY ABORTIONS WITH HIS BEARD.

Chuck Norris's ant farm is the third-highest producer of grain in the Midwest.

Chuck Norris won a staring contest with Medusa.

Chuck Norris's full legal name is Carlos Danger de Saavedra Sixth Duke of Atlantis Death Rattle degli Alighieri Ray Hohenzollern Saxe-Coburg and Gotha, Supreme Underwater Commando, Protector of the Second Amendment Norris.

CHUCK NORRIS IS THE HIGHEST-PAID MODEL IN HUNGARY.

The heavens parted, the seas quieted, the earth stood still. From her womb, the goddess brought forth Chuck Norris, sired by the sun, as a gift to mankind. He reclined upon the fertile soil under the crescent moon and immediately sprouted a beard. She spoke softly to the young child and said, "Go forth and roundhouse kick people in the face." So it was spoken, and so he does. Every now and then he also sells exercise equipment and wears awesome clothes.

When Chuck Norris has a good idea, he raises a forklift carrying a pallet of lightbulbs over his head.

CHUCK NORRIS DRIVES A PICKUP TRUCK UPHOLSTERED IN DENIM.

Chuck Norris choked an estimated four hundred thousand Vietcong to death in 1985.

CHUCK NORRIS WILL ONLY SEND LETTERS IN ENVELOPES MADE OF CHAIN MAIL.

CHUCK NORRIS CAN HAVE AN ALL-YOU-CAN-EAT BUFFET DELIVERED.

Chuck Norris was captain of the Love Boat until one day when everyone woke up and saw they were in Pyongyang.

Chuck Norris swears he didn't sleep with your wife. Yes, it is strange that your children show an affinity for Texas justice and beard cultivation. No, Chuck Norris does not know why your wife can only climax when you wear a karate uniform. Chuck Norris thinks you are asking the kind of questions a person asks when they want to be roundhouse kicked in the face.

THE SAFEST SEX CHUCK NORRIS CAN GET IS WITH A VOLVO.

Chuck Norris is sharp enough to cut a tin can in half and can slice a tomato paper-thin.

Chuck Norris won a spelling bee by filling the judges' pants with a thousand angry wasps.

CHUCK NORRIS'S TEMPER IS DIRECTLY PROPORTIONAL TO THE NUMBER OF EPISODES OF *JERSEY SHORE*.

Chuck Norris's fallout shelter contains four hundred cans of Spam, thirty cases of Johnnie Walker Red, and six Total Gyms.

Chuck Norris will never shoot unarmed teenagers from Florida unless they're carrying Twizzlers; nobody should have to suffer through eating licorice.

CHUCK NORRIS'S REFRIGERATOR CAN KEEP MILK FRESH LONGER THAN MOST RELATIONSHIPS LAST.

Chuck Norris carries a midget in his pocket—after Chuck kicks ass, the midget takes names.

Chuck Norris took my virginity, and he will sure as hell take yours. If you're thinking to yourself, *"That's impossible, I already lost my virginity,"* then you are dead wrong.

CHUCK NORRIS CAN GRATE FRESH PARMESAN CHEESE WITH HIS RUST-RED BEARD.

Chuck Norris fought Gandhi in the very first Ultimate Fighting Championship and won in less than fifteen seconds by crushing Gandhi's rib cage with a single punch. Later, officials questioned the validity of the match, as it took place in Gandhi's home, while he was asleep.

CHUCK NORRIS WAS A 1981 *CONSUMER REPORTS* BEST BUY IN SNOWPLOWS.

Conspiracy theorists are skeptical of the 9/11 attack on the Pentagon because the damage looks awfully similar to the destruction left by Chuck Norris when he destroyed the Hexagon, Trapezoid, and Parallelogram buildings.

CHUCK NORRIS CAN WIN A LOSE-LOSE SITUATION.

Contrary to popular belief, Chuck Norris, not the blue-ringed octopus of eastern Australia, is the most venomous creature on earth. Within three minutes of being bitten, a human being experiences the following symptoms: fever, blurred vision, beard rash, tightness of the jeans, and the feeling of being repeatedly kicked through a car windshield.

IN CHUCK NORRIS'S HOMELAND, A ROUNDHOUSE KICK TO THE FACE IS EQUIVALENT TO A HANDSHAKE.

The only way Chuck Norris can climax is if there's a Vietnamese family begging for their lives nearby.

CHUCK NORRIS'S FAVORITE POWER LUNCH IS A DOZEN NINE-VOLT BATTERIES.

CHUCK NORRIS'S FIRST WORDS WERE THE OPENING SPEECH FROM *PATTON*.

To be more environmentally conscious, Chuck Norris retrofitted his pickup truck to run on Toyota Priuses.

If you ever get Chuck Norris's voice mail, the greeting will be, "Hello. I am not available to take your call right now **BECAUSE I AM IN YOUR HOUSE.**"

Chuck Norris once competed in a celebrity edition of the game show *The Weakest Link* that went to sudden death. There were fourteen casualties.

Chuck Norris's left testicle was declared the Milky Way's tenth planet in 1978. His right testicle remains the Duke of the Thirteenth Republic of South Greenwich.

CHUCK NORRIS USED TO BE A REGULAR GUEST ON *SESAME STREET*, UNTIL SNUFFLEUPAGUS ACCIDENTALLY ATE CHUCK'S SANDWICH. MANY MUPPETS DIED THAT DAY.

At one crossroad in his life, Chuck Norris considered becoming an obstetrician and a postman so he could deliver newborns by mail.

Chuck Norris's portrait has killed more visitors than any other painting in the history of the Smithsonian National Portrait Gallery.

HANG TOUGH CHUCK

Every summer, Chuck Norris invites the remaining cast members of *The Partridge Family* and *The Brady Bunch* to a fight to the death inside an active volcano.

CHUCK NORRIS'S NIPPLES CAN BE MILKED FOR THE SMOOTHEST FORTY-YEAR-AGED TEXAS WHISKEY YOU WILL EVER TASTE.

The last time Chuck Norris went to a karaoke bar, he sang Lee Greenwood's "God Bless the USA" and the next day was awarded the Congressional Medal of Honor.

In an alternate universe, the clean-shaven Chuck Norris of the 1970s is engaged in an epic battle with the bearded Chuck Norris of the eighties and nineties. The result of this conflict is the aurora borealis.

CHUCK NORRIS CARVED MOUNT RUSHMORE OVERNIGHT, BY HIMSELF WITH HIS TEETH.

Chuck Norris's beard glows red when he proves a syllogism.

The lightbulbs in Chuck Norris's house are replaced every day because nobody wants to run the risk of getting stuck in the dark with Chuck Norris.

CHUCK NORRIS'S ROUNDHOUSE KICKS HAVE BROKEN OVER ONE MILLION BONES, BUT HIS SMILE HAS BROKEN TEN TIMES AS MANY HEARTS.

Chuck Norris once delivered a performance so stiff that a cameraman was later pulled over for DWI.

Chuck Norris has a birthmark in the shape of Chuck Norris kicking a ninja.

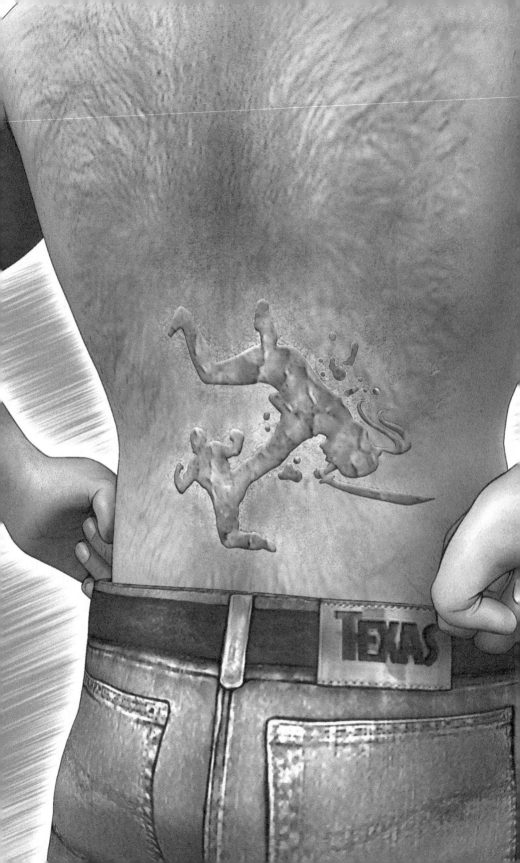

When you look back and see only one set of footprints, that's when Chuck Norris was carrying you.

THE ONLY REASON WORLD WAR II OCCURRED WAS BECAUSE CHUCK NORRIS WAS TAKING A NAP.

If you unscramble the letters in "Chuck Norris" you get "Huck corn, sir." That is why every fall Chuck travels to Nebraska and burns the entire state down.

Chuck Norris roundhouse kicked Jimmy Hoffa into the future. In the year 2052, Hoffa will reappear and crash through the windshield of a flying car.

CHUCK NORRIS EATS BABIES AND SHITS DELTA FORCE TEAM MEMBERS.

CHUCK NORRIS GARGLES WITH ANTIFREEZE.

Chuck Norris took three of every animal on his ark. Then he called Noah a pussy and roundhouse kicked a Minotaur.

CHUCK NORRIS WAS ONE OF THE ORIGINAL MEMBERS OF WU-TANG CLAN, BUT QUIT BECAUSE THEY WEREN'T STREET ENOUGH.

Chuck Norris had sex with your mom, and your dad gave him a high five.

If the coach had put Chuck Norris in in the fourth quarter, they would have won State. No doubt about it.

CHUCK NORRIS CAN SLAM
A REVOLVING DOOR.

Chuck Norris maintains his beard to keep the radar units in his face working at the optimal temperature.

CHUCK NORRIS'S BEARD HAS A REPRESENTATIVE IN CONGRESS.

Chuck Norris owns a cell phone that can only make and receive calls from Shepard Smith.

Chuck Norris pronounces "ballet" like "ballot," "Arkansas" like "are-Kansas," and "Barack Obama" like "Kenyan socialist."

If looks could kill, Chuck Norris would have gouged out one of his eyes years ago just to make it challenging.

CHUCK NORRIS ENDS EVERY RELATIONSHIP WITH, "IT'S NOT ME, IT'S YOU."

The movie *Rambo: First Blood* was inspired by Chuck Norris's experiences as a Boy Scout.

The Obama administration originally wanted to send Chuck Norris to clean up the BP oil spill, but they axed the idea after hearing a rumor that crude oil only makes Chuck Norris stronger.

Upon arriving on the moon, Neil Armstrong caught a 382,500-kilometer touchdown pass from Chuck Norris.

CHUCK NORRIS IS SO FERTILE THAT WHEN HE BANGS A CHICK IN AMERICA, A CHICK IN CHINA GETS PREGNANT.

Chuck Norris refuses to see *The Social Network* because he's had five hundred million friends since 1972.

CHUCK NORRIS'S STORM CELLAR CONTAINS A TUNNEL THAT LEADS YOU DIRECTLY TO SYDNEY, AUSTRALIA.

In a direct-to-DVD sequel to the animated classic, Chuck Norris plays the eighth dwarf, Murdery, who bangs Snow White.

Despite his doctor's and family's strong objections, Chuck Norris began drinking gasoline each morning. Much to everyone's surprise, he gets ninety-four miles per gallon.

CHUCK NORRIS'S PUBIC HAIR IS TWICE AS THICK AS HIS BEARD... BUT NOT NEARLY AS DEADLY.

Chuck Norris won a People's Choice Award for winning a knife fight against Joe Biden.

CHUCK NORRIS CALLS 411 EVERY DAY AT NOON ASKING FOR THE LATEST UPDATES ON THE SOVIETS.

Emperor Nero paid Chuck Norris sacks of gold and silver to burn Rome to the ground. Chuck Norris accepted because that buys a lot of whey powder.

A man once asked Chuck Norris if his real name is "Charles." Chuck Norris did not respond, he simply stared at him until the man exploded.

THE VIETNAM WAR ENDED OVER THIRTY YEARS AGO. NOBODY TOLD CHUCK NORRIS.

Alien vs. Predator is an autobiographical depiction of Chuck Norris's first sexual experience.

Every scene from *Life* and *Planet Earth* was filmed in Chuck Norris's pants.

CHUCK NORRIS ONCE RIPPED A MAN IN HALF JUST TO SEE WHAT HE HAD FOR LUNCH.

Chuck Norris spent an entire month jumping off high-rise buildings intending to marry the first woman who could catch him.

Chuck Norris can tell the difference between Pepsi and RC Cola, but he has yet to use this skill.

Chuck Norris had seven children. Four of them went on to become doctors. The other three were delicious.

A MASKED MAN ONCE STABBED CHUCK NORRIS IN AN ALLEY BEHIND A CHILDREN'S HOSPITAL. THE KNIFE BLED TO DEATH.

Terrorists recently attempted to hijack Chuck Norris's private plane. This resulted in the world record for farthest distance a cowboy boot has been stuck up someone's ass.

CHUCK NORRIS HAS GOOD REASONS TO BELIEVE THAT MARY WAS, IN FACT, NOT A VIRGIN.

Chuck Norris called GEICO and in fifteen minutes saved fifteen senior citizens from a blazing building before convincing the phone representative to donate $10,000 to the Republican Party.

Chuck Norris and his brother cracked four of Bob Barker's ribs while teaching him karate. Read that again because it is actually true.

The Swedish invented IKEA so they could spend less time building furniture and more time running from Chuck Norris and his deep displeasure with the Bauhaus style and European modernism.

Chuck Norris once roundhouse kicked Bruce Lee, breaking him in half. The result was Jet Li and Jackie Chan.

CHUCK NORRIS REFEREED A DUEL BETWEEN GENERAL TSO AND COLONEL SANDERS.

Some sideshow performers can look at a person and tell them their birthday. Chuck Norris can look at a person and tell them when they will die.

WHEN CHUCK NORRIS PLAYS BASKETBALL, HIS DICK GETS ITS OWN JERSEY AND USUALLY PLAYS FOR THE OPPOSING TEAM.

Chuck Norris stuffs his Thanksgiving turkey with a forty-eight-ounce porterhouse steak stuffed inside a Vietnamese prison guard.

THE ONLY THING ABLE TO CUT CHUCK NORRIS'S BEARD IS HIS RAZOR-SHARP REFLEXES.

Chuck Norris's favorite hot dog topping is mustard distilled from the tears of the children of his victims. Chuck Norris eats a lot of hot dogs.

A single hair from Chuck Norris's beard is soft enough to be woven into the softest bedsheets you will ever sleep on, yet strong enough to suspend Wilford Brimley in gale-force winds.

The Total Gym can also grill cheeseburgers, press your pants, and file your taxes, and Chuck Norris can teach you how on twelve incredible DVDs for just seven easy payments of $39.95.

CHUCK NORRIS ONCE TOBOGGANED DOWN MOUNT EVEREST AND SPRINTED BACK TO THE TOP WHEN HE REALIZED HE HAD LOST HIS MITTENS.

If Chuck Norris looks at you and even *thinks* about Jesus, you are immediately converted to Christianity.

CHUCK NORRIS'S UNDERWEAR CAN RESIST CONTINUOUS GUNFIRE FOR UP TO TWENTY-FOUR HOURS.

Chuck Norris's most prized possession is his signed copy of the 1993 Women of the U.S. Attorney's Office commemorative wall calendar.

CHUCK NORRIS ONLY ALLOWS
JACKIE CHAN TO LIVE BECAUSE
HE LIKES CHRIS TUCKER MOVIES.

CHUCK NORRIS OWNS AND OPERATES HIS OWN RESTAURANT IN LUBBOCK, TEXAS. KNUCKLE SANDWICHES ARE THE ONLY THING ON THE MENU.

Similar to a Russian nesting doll, if you were to break Chuck Norris open you would find another Chuck Norris inside, only smaller and angrier.

CHUCK NORRIS'S GENES AREN'T A DOUBLE HELIX. THEY'RE BARBED WIRE.

Tony Stark made an Iron Man suit for Chuck Norris, but Chuck has never used it because it only slows him down.

The only papers WikiLeaks have on Chuck Norris just have "Fuck you, Dan Rather" written on them in blood.

CHUCK NORRIS USES THE SAME OCTANE GASOLINE IN HIS CAR, LAWN MOWER, AND MARTINIS.

Chuck Norris takes a baseball bat into the bathroom with him in case he craps out a wildcat and has to beat it to death.

CHUCK NORRIS CAN PUT A QUARTER IN HIS ASS AND THEN SHIT OUT A DIME AND TWO NICKELS. THERE IS A FIVE-CENT CHARGE.

Chuck Norris's plan for Middle East peace is to airdrop Total Gyms for every man, woman, and child across the entire region until there are no more complaints.

When Chuck Norris sends in his taxes, he mails blank forms and includes only a picture of himself, crouched and ready to attack. Chuck Norris has not had to pay taxes ever.

CHUCK NORRIS'S FAVORITE BOND GIRL IS THE TANK FROM *GOLDENEYE*.

THE LAST PERSON CHUCK NORRIS BLEW OUT OF THE WATER DIED FROM THE BENDS.

You can find Chuck Norris at Costco, Walmart, or any retailer where firearms, power tools, knives, duct tape, Vaseline, and Fritos are sold.

CHUCK NORRIS'S PENIS IS SO MASSIVE THAT IT HAS ITS OWN ELBOW.

If a tree falls in the middle of a forest and no one is anywhere around, rest assured that Chuck Norris heard it.

If you ask Chuck Norris what time it is, he always says, "Two seconds till." After you ask, "Two seconds till what?" he roundhouse kicks you in the face.

Chuck Norris caused the *Hindenburg* to erupt in flames upon landing as a warning to travelers to stay away from New Jersey.

HITCH YOUR WAGON TO A STAR, UNLESS THAT STAR HAPPENS TO BE CHUCK NORRIS, IN WHICH CASE YOU PROBABLY OUGHT TO CONSIDER AN ALTERNATE CAREER.

When he retires, Chuck Norris plans to become a police officer and partner up with Steven Seagal, finally melding justice and confusion in a way previously thought by experts to be impossible.

WHEN CHUCK NORRIS WANTS A FANCY BREAKFAST, HE ORDERS A FABERGÉ OMELET.

As a good Christian, Chuck Norris ought to forgive anyone for wrongdoings against him. Unfortunately, Chuck Norris retains Jewish attorneys, so good luck with that.

A massive avalanche in the Kohistan District of Pakistan in February 2010 killed over one hundred people. Coincidentally, it occurred at the exact instant that Chuck Norris heard about plans for an Islamic cultural center blocks from Ground Zero.

CHUCK NORRIS IS ALL FOR GOVERNMENT BAILOUTS SO LONG AS REPAYMENT IS ENFORCED BY DOG THE BOUNTY HUNTER.

Chuck Norris can turn back time simply by staring at the clock and flexing.

Chuck Norris's semen cures AIDS but causes Alzheimer's disease. HIV-positive women he bangs live for a long time, but they don't remember why.

CHUCK NORRIS'S DOG IS TRAINED TO PICK UP HIS OWN POOP BECAUSE CHUCK NORRIS WILL NOT TAKE SHIT FROM ANYONE.

The Good, The Bad, and The Ugly are Chuck Norris's nicknames for his testicles.

THE SYMBOL FOR CHUCK NORRIS IN SIGN LANGUAGE IS A MIDDLE FINGER ON FIRE.

If you stare at the American flag long enough, a 3-D image of Chuck Norris pops up.

CHUCK NORRIS ONCE KILLED A MAN BY SIMPLY SHOWING HIM HOW TO LOVE.

Chuck Norris's first solution for the cholera outbreak in Haiti was another earthquake.

CHUCK NORRIS TOOK GARY COLEMAN TO SMALL CLAIMS COURT JUST FOR THE IRONY.

As a young man, Chuck Norris wore the pants in every relationship he was in to the point where he refused to let his girlfriend even own pants.

Chuck Norris's last option is violence. It is also his only option.

Chuck Norris likes his girls like he likes his whiskey—twelve years old and mixed up with coke.

THERE IS NO CHIN BEHIND CHUCK NORRIS'S BEARD. THERE IS ONLY ANOTHER FIST.

IN 2008, CHUCK NORRIS WON THE FINA WATER POLO WORLD LEAGUE TOURNAMENT ENTIRELY ON HORSEBACK.

Chuck Norris won the Triple Crown last year for the first time since 1978. He needed no horse.

JESUS OWNS AND WEARS A BRACELET THAT READS, "WWCND?"

Chuck Norris once put a thousand monkeys at a thousand typewriters for a thousand years to see if they would, in fact, turn out the complete works of Shakespeare. Unfortunately, they were only able to compose the screenplay for *Delta Force 2: The Colombian Connection.*

Contrary to popular belief, Justice isn't blind. **CHUCK NORRIS IS JUST THE ONLY PERSON SHE WANTS TO SEE.**

THE QUICKEST WAY TO A MAN'S HEART IS WITH CHUCK NORRIS'S FIST.

Chuck Norris was inducted into the Baseball Hall of Fame for ordering a Denny's Grand Slam breakfast combo.

CHE GUEVARA WAS BURIED WEARING A SHIRT WITH CHUCK NORRIS ON IT.

Every dinosaur skull ever found has the imprint of a size fifteen cowboy boot on its jaw. Scientists are baffled, but we know damn well why.

CHUCK NORRIS LOST HIS VIRGINITY BEFORE HIS DAD DID.

Chuck Norris can sing a solo in perfect three-part harmony.

Chuck Norris can win a three-legged race by himself.

CHUCK NORRIS IS NOT HUNG LIKE A HORSE . . . HORSES ARE HUNG LIKE CHUCK NORRIS.

Never try to return a Chuck Norris Total Gym. Within sixty seconds of the thought entering your mind, Chuck Norris will rappel through your living-room window, scissor-kick you in the throat, and immediately power-fuck Christie Brinkley on your Total Gym.

Chuck Norris went as Chuck Norris for Halloween. He got twice as much candy as anybody else.

CHUCK NORRIS'S FIRST COLORING BOOK WAS THE *KAMA SUTRA*.

CHUCK NORRIS CALLS OUT HIS OWN NAME DURING SEX BECAUSE ANYTHING ELSE WOULD RUIN THE MOMENT.

Chuck Norris has no sense of self-preservation except for when he's making a batch of his award-winning jams.

After completing the act of love with Chuck Norris, many women find justice running down their inner thighs.

IF CHUCK NORRIS EVER TELLS YOU HE "FEELS LIKE MEXICAN TONIGHT," DON'T BE SURPRISED IF YOU HAPPEN TO FIND HIM SCREWING YOUR HOUSEKEEPER LATER THAT EVENING.

CHUCK NORRIS'S BEARD CONQUERED POLAND THREE TIMES.

Filming on location for *Walker, Texas Ranger,* Chuck Norris brought a stillborn baby lamb back to life by giving it a prolonged beard rub. Shortly after the farm animal sprang back to life and a crowd had gathered, Chuck Norris roundhouse kicked the animal, breaking its neck, to remind the crew once more that the good Chuck giveth, and the good Chuck, he taketh away.

Someone once tried to tell Chuck Norris that roundhouse kicks aren't the best way to kick someone. This has been recorded by historians as the worst mistake anyone has ever made.

CHUCK NORRIS TATTOOED HIS NAME ON HIS FIST SO IT WOULD BE THE LAST THING HIS VICTIMS SAW.

CHUCK NORRIS CAN
RECITE PI BACKWARD.

Before Chuck Norris came to Middle-earth, Hobbits were twelve feet tall.

Chuck Norris was the first person to reach the North Pole **BY ELEVATOR**.

CHUCK NORRIS ALWAYS GIVES HIS SEAT TO PREGNANT WOMEN ON THE TRAIN BUT NEVER APOLOGIZES FOR GETTING THEM PREGNANT.

Chuck Norris goes to the gun range so the targets can practice running from him.

FREDDY KRUEGER HAS NIGHTMARES ABOUT CHUCK NORRIS.

Chuck Norris's beard hit .370 in the minors before hurting its knee.

WHEN CHUCK NORRIS GOES TO THE BATHROOM, HE DOESN'T TAKE A SHIT, HE GIVES A SHIT.

The movie *King Kong* is loosely based on an incident in which Chuck Norris killed a nine-hundred-foot gorilla and had sex with the Coors Light twins on the top of the Empire State Building.

Good fences make good neighbors, but since Chuck Norris's neighbors couldn't afford a steel-reinforced replica of the Great Wall of China, they bake him fresh cookies every day.

CHUCK NORRIS DOESN'T USE TWITTER BECAUSE NOBODY CAN FOLLOW CHUCK NORRIS AND SURVIVE.

"B.C." ACTUALLY STANDS FOR "BEFORE CHUCK."

Chuck Norris designed the first Ed Hardy T-shirt when he ran out of douchebags to kill.

CHUCK NORRIS'S GINGER ALE IS MADE FROM 100 PERCENT PURE GINGER CHILDREN.

Chuck Norris's beard is that orange-brown color because that's what metal looks like when it's been exposed to the elements for too long.

Chuck Norris kicked a fifty-yard field goal while having sex.

CHUCK NORRIS'S MUG JUST SAYS "WORLD'S BEST."

What happens in Vegas stays in Vegas. Unless it was a Chuck Norris roundhouse kick to the face. That shit stays with you for life.

CHUCK NORRIS INVENTED THE MUFFIN WHEN HE WANTED A CUPCAKE FOR BREAKFAST.

One time in an airport, a guy accidentally called Chuck Norris "Chick Norris." He explained it was an honest mistake and apologized profusely. Chuck accepted his apology and politely signed an autograph. Nine months later, the guy's wife gave birth to a bearded baby. The guy knew exactly what had happened, and blames nobody but himself.

Chuck Norris does not have normal male nipples. He has a Dodge Ram hood ornament on each pec, and both rams blow smoke out of their noses each and every time he pumps Christie Brinkley.

TWO ROADS DIVERGED IN A YELLOW WOOD BECAUSE CHUCK NORRIS TOLD THEM TO.

When, as a child, he was placed on Santa Claus's lap for a photo, Chuck Norris shat out Donner, Blitzen, and four other reindeer.

On the first day, God created the heavens and the earth, looked down, and then said, "Holy shit, is that Chuck Norris?"

CHUCK NORRIS WIPES WITH FORTY-GRIT SANDPAPER.

Somewhere, right now, Chuck Norris is plowing a woman he doesn't love.

Chuck Norris went to college on an affirmative-action scholarship. Nobody objected.

THE GREEK PRONUNCIATION OF CHUCK NORRIS IS ZEUS.

A blind man once stepped on Chuck Norris's shoe. Chuck said, "Don't you know who I am? I'm Chuck Norris!" The mere mention of his name cured this man's blindness. Sadly the first, last, and only thing this man ever saw was a fatal roundhouse kick delivered by Chuck Norris.

Chuck Norris is one-eighth Cherokee. This has nothing to do with ancestry; the man ate a fucking Indian.

CHUCK NORRIS WATERBOARDS HIMSELF TO CLEAR HIS SINUSES.

There is no comeback for an insult from Chuck Norris. Then again, if Chuck Norris wanted some comeback, he would have asked your mom for it.

The saddest moment for a child is not when she learns Santa Claus isn't real, it's when she learns Chuck Norris is.

**CHUCK NORRIS DOESN'T SPEAK. HE
THINKS WORDS TOWARD HIS FOOT
AND THEN ROUNDHOUSE KICKS THEM
AT YOUR BRAIN.**

Chuck Norris uses **ENTIRE BOOKS** as bookmarks.

Chuck Norris invented napalm as a hand cream long
before anyone used it in war.

WHEN YOU OPEN A CAN OF WHOOP-ASS, CHUCK NORRIS JUMPS OUT.

The grass is always greener on the other side, unless
Chuck Norris has been there. In that case the grass is
most likely soaked in blood and tears.

Chuck Norris owns a Swiss Army knife that contains a colander, a flamethrower, and a Snuggie.

EVERY ROOM IN CHUCK NORRIS'S HOUSE IS A PANIC ROOM.

Chuck Norris's immune system is
MORE EFFICIENT THAN AN INDONESIAN SWEATSHOP.

Chuck Norris's entry in *The Hitchhiker's Guide to the Galaxy* reads simply, "Panic."

CHUCK NORRIS'S WEEK IS ONLY SIX DAYS LONG BECAUSE HE REFUSES TO RECOGNIZE TUESDAY.

MEN ARE FROM MARS AND WOMEN ARE FROM VENUS, BUT CHUCK NORRIS IS FROM THE UNITED STATES OF AMERICA, SO MEN AND WOMEN CAN GO FUCK THEMSELVES.

On a good day, there is another side of Chuck Norris, a gentler, more feminine side. Chuck Norris hasn't had any good days yet.

Chuck Norris owns a compass that always points in the direction of Sean Hannity.

CHUCK NORRIS WAS THE FIRST TO INSTALL A FIREPLACE IN AN IGLOO.

Chuck Norris once got 100 percent on a calculus exam by writing "violence" for every question. Chuck Norris solves all problems with violence.

It's a little known fact that only three things will survive the apocalypse: cockroaches, Chuck Norris, and Chuck Norris's beard.

CHUCK NORRIS ONCE ATE AN ENTIRE FACTORY OF SLEEPING PILLS. THEY MADE HIM BLINK.

Chuck Norris coached a vending machine to win a speed skating tournament.

People who live in glass houses shouldn't throw stones unless they're positive that Chuck Norris is nowhere nearby and would be highly unlikely to ever catch wind of the incident.

The leopard does not change his spots, but Chuck Norris changes out of his leopard-skin thongs often enough to keep them smelling presentable.

CHUCK NORRIS BELIEVES IN TROUT.

CHUCK NORRIS ONCE ROUNDHOUSE KICKED CANCER SO HARD HE GAVE IT AIDS.

Imitation is the sincerest form of flattery, but imitation of Chuck Norris will only get you flattened.

The opera ain't over till the fat lady sings or Chuck Norris decapitates the chorus, which turns out to have been goons from the Japanese Yakuza in disguise.

WHEN CHUCK NORRIS TAKES A SHOWER, THE LEFTOVER WATER IS 68 PERCENT ALCOHOL BY VOLUME.

Newspapers have been going out of business because Chuck Norris finally switched to toilet paper.

There's none so blind as those who will not see, except for those whose eyes have been forced from their skulls by a scissor kick to the temple from Chuck Norris.

A kid once stole Chuck Norris's hat and ran into an apple orchard. Chuck Norris flew into such a rage that he accidentally invented applesauce.

CHUCK NORRIS INVENTED THE WATER BED AFTER HIS FIRST WET DREAM.

CHUCK NORRIS DOES NOT HANG UP ON PEOPLE; HE JUST HANGS THEM.

Chuck Norris can create a rock so heavy that even he can't lift it. And then he lifts it anyway, just to show you who the fuck Chuck Norris is.

Chuck Norris was asked to resign from the Weather Channel for only forecasting "destruction."

e
ather
annel

ORECAST

TOTALLY
FUCKED

Chuck Norris feels your pain as an explosion of anger directed at your face.

THE VIRGIN MARY SAW CHUCK NORRIS IN HER GRILLED CHEESE SANDWICH.

Chuck Norris is a conservative; he understands the need to conserve his energy to kick as many liberal asses as possible.

Chuck Norris has settled every case brought against him by offering the aggrieved party a single hair from his beard.

CHUCK NORRIS HAS SIRED A KENTUCKY DERBY CHAMPION AND ITS JOCKEY.

Chuck Norris's friends with benefits have the benefit of not being his enemies.

Chuck Norris's orgasm has been known to trigger avalanches throughout Europe, volcanic eruptions around the Pacific Rim, and violent political unrest across Tatooine.

THE ONLY THING CHUCK NORRIS EVER LOST WAS HIS VIRGINITY.

IF YOU KNOW SOMEONE WHO DOESN'T LIKE CHUCK NORRIS, YOU WON'T KNOW THEM FOR LONG.

The day Chuck Norris sleeps with your wife is the happiest day of your life.

The devil once secretly replaced Chuck Norris's immortal soul with Folgers crystals. Chuck Norris couldn't tell the difference.

CHUCK NORRIS FLOSSES WITH BARBED WIRE.

In his recent biography, President George W. Bush admits that he never invaded Iran because Chuck Norris told him, "Leave that one for me."

Blood is thicker than water, **EXCEPT FOR THE WATER IN CHUCK NORRIS'S TEAR DUCTS**, which have petrified into diamonds from decades of disuse.

Appearances are deceptive. Most people assume Chuck Norris can chew through steel; this is true, but only because his lava-like saliva renders it quite soft.

CHUCK NORRIS SNORES IN IAMBIC PENTAMETER.

Chuck Norris blew up the *Challenger* space shuttle. When asked why, he said, "I've never left a challenger alive."

WHEN FILLING OUT A JOB APPLICATION, CHUCK NORRIS FILLS IN HIS RACE AS "SUPERIOR."

For fun, Chuck Norris likes to visit veterinary hospitals. When asked if he has a sick pet, Chuck Norris flexes his biceps and says, "These pythons are pretty sick." He then kisses his arms until all the ladies explode with orgasmic fury.

Chuck Norris does not hunt because the word **"HUNTING"** implies the possibility of failure. Chuck Norris goes killing.

The original title for *Alien vs. Predator* was *Alien and Predator vs. Chuck Norris*. The film was canceled shortly after going into preproduction. No one would pay nine dollars to see a movie fourteen seconds long.

There is no theory of evolution, only a list of creatures that Chuck Norris has allowed to live.

CHUCK NORRIS HATES WALL STREET FAT CATS, BUT HE LOVES HOW THEY TASTE IN STEWS.

To reach the front door of Chuck Norris's house, you must cross a moat on the night of a new moon, tunnel precisely 32.6 meters beneath the earth, answer the gorgon's sixteen riddles in ancient Greek, cross a burning rope bridge hundreds of feet above a river of burning lava, and avoid the fighting colonies of irradiated soldier ants. And if you get past the land mines, the door is unlocked.

Chuck Norris plays the castanets by checking himself for testicular cancer.

WHENEVER CHUCK NORRIS'S WIFE ASKS HIM NICELY TO DO THE DISHES, HE THROWS THEM IN THE GARBAGE AND TELLS HER SHE LOOKS FAT.

A handicap parking sign does not signify that the spot is for handicapped people. It is actually in fact a warning that the spot belongs to Chuck Norris and that you will be handicapped if you park there.

CHUCK NORRIS CAN HEAL A HEAD WOUND WITH HIS THOUGHTS.

Chuck Norris turned down the chance to play James Bond because the weapons took all the fun out of the killing.

Edward and Jacob are on Team Chuck.

**CHUCK NORRIS CAN IGNORE THE CALL
OF NATURE FOR UP TO THIRTY-SIX HOURS,
BUT HE CAN NEVER IGNORE THE CALL OF DUTY.**

A reporter once asked Chuck Norris what was on his mind; Chuck Norris removed the top of his skull, bent down to display his brain matter, and then replaced his pate.

CHUCK NORRIS ONCE SWALLOWED A PYTHON TO GET TO THE LIVE DEER IN ITS STOMACH.

Chuck Norris supports debt relief. He believes people should be comfortable before he kills them.

Chuck Norris once played Jenga. The result was the Empire State Building.

CHUCK NORRIS KILLS VAMPIRES SIMPLY BY CROSSING HIS FINGERS.

If Chuck Norris is ever disappointed with his writing, he crumples up his monitor and throws it away.

Only God has the authority to edit Chuck Norris's Wikipedia page.

GEORGE CLOONEY IS STILL SINGLE BECAUSE HE'S HOLDING OUT FOR CHUCK NORRIS.

Whitney Houston died because Chuck Norris can only live in a world with one Houston.

When God and Satan play a game of football, Chuck Norris is the field they play upon.

Chuck Norris waited patiently in Al Capone's vault for sixty-three years just so he could give Geraldo Rivera the surprise beating of his lifetime.

CHUCK NORRIS'S LUCKY BASEBALL BAT IS ACTUALLY A LIVE BOA CONSTRICTOR STUFFED TO THE BRIM WITH MICE.

Nintendo changed *Chuck Norris's Punch-Out!!* to *Mike Tyson's Punch-Out!!* because of complaints that the last level was unbeatable.

WHEN CHUCK NORRIS COVERS HIS EYES DURING PEEKABOO, BABIES DISAPPEAR FOREVER.

When a Chuck Norris movie bombs, an average of 323 people die in the aftermath.

HOW MUCH WOOD WOULD A WOODCHUCK CHUCK IF A WOODCHUCK COULD CHUCK NORRIS? ALL OF IT.

At Chuck Norris's circumcision, doctors ran through five diamond-studded chain saws before giving up.

The movie *Hellraiser* is based on real-life events that occurred after someone tried to solve the Chuck Norris: Karate Kommandos Special Edition Rubik's Cube.

CHUCK NORRIS'S CHILDREN WERE BORN FULLY BEARDED.

If the axiom, "You are what you eat" is true, then Chuck Norris is a combination of monster truck tires, Godzilla, and magma from the earth's most active volcanoes.

CHUCK NORRIS CLOGS THE TOILET EVEN WHEN HE PISSES.

CHUCK NORRIS'S MONEY SHOT CAN ACTUALLY BE COUNTED IN TENS AND TWENTIES.

Chuck Norris stalked, captured, killed, and ate his own shadow because it was working for the KGB.

The Irish Potato Famine started when Chuck Norris had a hankering for latkes.

ONLY WONDER WOMAN HAS A UTERUS CAPABLE OF BEARING CHUCK NORRIS'S CHILDREN.

Chuck Norris eats tiger hearts every morning for strength, power, and wisdom. He eats men's hearts for sport.

WHEN CHUCK NORRIS RAISES HIS EYEBROWS, MATING SEASON BEGINS AROUND THE WORLD.

Chuck Norris uses a hollowed-out elephant trunk as a holster for his penis.

In order to survive a nuclear attack, you must remember to stop, drop, and be Chuck Norris.

CHUCK NORRIS FREQUENTLY DONATES BLOOD TO THE RED CROSS. JUST NEVER HIS OWN.

All Chuck Norris wants for Christmas is your two front teeth.

CHUCK NORRIS SWEATS THE FORCE.

The *Cloud Gate* sculpture in Chicago's Millennium Park is on loan from Chuck Norris's scrotum.

The North Korean army once lost a battle against a signed Chuck Norris poster.

There are two kinds of people in this world: people who are Chuck Norris and people who are going to die.

CHUCK NORRIS REMEMBERS THE ALAMO, AND HE ISN'T HAPPY ABOUT IT.

Chuck Norris is the only signatory to the laws of nature.

CHUCK NORRIS'S PENIS HAS A LICENSE TO THRILL.

Chuck Norris trained an army of zombies to defend themselves against a robot uprising.

OZZY OSBOURNE ONCE BIT THE HEAD
OFF A BAT. NOT TO BE OUTDONE,
CHUCK NORRIS THEN BIT THE HEAD
OFF BATMAN.

EVERY PUNCH CHUCK NORRIS THROWS HITS THE STRIKE ZONE.

In 2008, Chuck Norris started an NGO to relieve Colombian drug cartels of their teeth.

ON SUBWAY CARS, THE CLOSING DOORS STAND CLEAR OF CHUCK NORRIS.

Chuck Norris solved the Bermuda triangle by using the Pythagorean theorem.

The Bible says Samson killed fifteen thousand Philistines with the jawbone of an ass. When God asked Chuck Norris what he thought about that, he said, "That's one way to do it." God laughed at Chuck's wisdom, and said, "I knew you were going to say that."

CHUCK NORRIS CAN FINISH OTHER PEOPLE'S SENTENCES WITH HIS FIST.

Chuck Norris brought an army of soldier ants to the brink of nuclear war.

The Rocky Mountains were created when Chuck Norris pushed California closer to Texas so his flights from Los Angeles to Dallas would take less time.

THE ORIGINAL CONCEPT FOR THE FILM *AMERICAN BEAUTY* WAS A SHIRTLESS CHUCK NORRIS SALUTING THE FLAG FOR TWO HOURS.

Chuck Norris is why Pat Sajak's talk show failed.

"THE LAND OF MILK AND HONEY" IS CHUCK NORRIS'S NICKNAME FOR HIS PECTORAL MUSCLES.

Chuck Norris is the only member of the U.S. Olympic transoceanic relay team.

Chuck Norris does the *New York Times* crossword puzzle **IN BLOOD.**

Chuck Norris can synchronize his urination with the fountains at the Bellagio.

Chuck Norris was supposed to be the next face on Mount Rushmore. Unfortunately granite is not a hard enough material to replicate Chuck Norris's beard.

Chuck Norris was once on a 747 that crashed. Even though rescue teams got to the wreckage within fifteen minutes, Chuck Norris had already eaten all the other survivors.

Lawyers at the studio behind *Walker, Texas Ranger* won't let them rerelease it in 3-D because of the certainty of millions of dollars in accidental-death lawsuit settlements.

WHEN CHUCK NORRIS'S SHIT HITS THE FAN, THE FAN BREAKS.

As a teen Chuck Norris impregnated every nun in a convent tucked away in the hills of Tuscany. Nine months later the nuns gave birth to the 1972 Miami Dolphins, the only undefeated and untied team in professional football history.

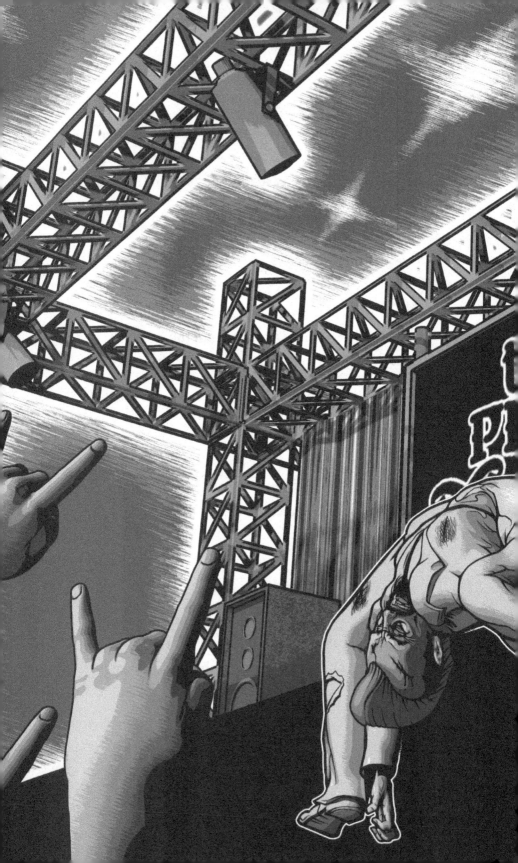

THE BLACK EYED PEAS WERE
SIMPLY KNOWN AS THE PEAS UNTIL
THEY CROSSED CHUCK NORRIS.

**MEMORIAL DAY IS A HOLIDAY WEEKEND
BECAUSE IT TAKES THREE DAYS TO READ A
LIST OF ALL OF CHUCK NORRIS'S VICTIMS.**

Moses's encounter with the burning bush was actually
a conversation with the pubic area of a woman Chuck
Norris had just boned.

SHAQUILLE O'NEAL WEARS CHUCK NORRIS'S BABY SHOES DURING GAMES.

Chuck Norris is so fast he can turn off his bedroom light
and be under the covers before the room gets dark.

Chuck Norris was the Jewish Humanitarian
of the Year. (Seriously.)

PETER PAN WANTS TO STAY A BOY BECAUSE HE CAN'T GROW UP TO BECOME CHUCK NORRIS.

Chuck Norris built the railroads with his own two hands, making tracks from shavings taken from his testicles.

AT ROCK CONCERTS, CHUCK NORRIS PLUGS HIS EARS WITH LIVE KITTENS.

When told to talk to the hand, Chuck Norris ripped it off and used it to judo-chop its original owner.

CHUCK NORRIS WON THE INDY 500 DRIVING A HARD BARGAIN.

CHUCK NORRIS COMBS HIS HAIR WITH THE TEETH OF A MIGHTY LION.

Chuck Norris is just like you and me: He puts his pants on one leg at a time. Except when he puts his pants on, he fights North Koreans.

The Snuggie was invented after someone saw Chuck Norris watch *Walker, Texas Ranger* while wearing the skin of a bear he had dressed himself.

CHUCK NORRIS DOESN'T GIVE CHRISTMAS PRESENTS. IF YOU LIVE TO SEE CHRISTMAS, THAT IS YOUR CHRISTMAS PRESENT FROM CHUCK.

Who are Chuck Norris's parents? Might, Justice, and Cunning. Yes, all three.

STATES THAT VOTE RED ARE VOTING FOR CHUCK NORRIS'S BEARD.

Chuck Norris kills people with kindness before killing them again with a roundhouse kick.

WHEN CHUCK NORRIS WORKS OUT, HE SWEATS FORTITUDE.

Chuck Norris only carries money so he can bet on himself.

TO SHOW ITS PATRIOTISM,
THE AMERICAN FLAG RECENTLY
GOT A TATTOO OF CHUCK NORRIS.

CHUCK NORRIS IS THE FIRST PERSON ON THE GHOSTBUSTERS' SPEED DIAL.

Chuck Norris has killed eighty-seven mimes with one invisible shotgun.

CHUCK NORRIS DONATES ALL PROCEEDS FROM THE TOTAL GYM TO HIS CHILDREN WITHOUT BEARDS FOUNDATION.

Chuck Norris once ordered a Big Mac at Burger King, and got one.

Pee-wee Herman once got arrested for masturbating in public. That same day, Chuck Norris got an award for masturbating in public.

Chuck Norris did not guest-star on *Seinfeld* because you always know what the deal with Chuck Norris is.

CHUCK NORRIS'S NICKNAME IS CHARLES.

Mormons keep high-quality genealogical records to prove that every member of their religion is descended from Chuck Norris.

CHUCK NORRIS TAUGHT A BEAR TO TRAIN A PACK OF WOLVES TO RAISE A HUMAN BOY.

When Chuck Norris enters a nightclub, he instantly becomes the life of the party. An instant is roughly how long it takes Chuck Norris to kill a room full of people.

CHUCK NORRIS COINCIDENTALLY LIVES IN A ROUND HOUSE.

Barbie left Ken for Chuck Norris and his one-twelfth-scale Jeep Wrangler but went back to Ken when she couldn't deal with Chuck Norris's full-scale penis.

CONAN O'BRIEN'S COIF IS MADE FROM HAIR SHAVED OFF CHUCK NORRIS'S BACK.

Chuck Norris holds the record for fastest lap speed around the Nürburgring in a pontoon boat dragged by a brontosaurus.

THE STATE OF KENTUCKY WAS FOUNDED BECAUSE CHUCK NORRIS NEEDED A PLACE TO HANG OUT.

Chuck Norris once punched a hole in a cow just to see what was coming up the road.

Chuck Norris tightrope walked across the Pacific Ocean, stopping only once, in Guam, to liberate it from the Spanish.

THE CONCEPT OF A GEOCENTRIC SOLAR SYSTEM MAKES CHUCK NORRIS SEXUALLY EXCITED.

Chuck Norris can tell when a woman is ovulating just by sticking his fist down her throat.

When visiting Hawaii, Chuck Norris always makes sure to have unprotected sex with a volcano.

CHUCK NORRIS'S IDEA OF A BALANCED DIET IS A FORTY-EIGHT-OUNCE STEAK IN EACH HAND.

A good way to tell if you are about to be attacked by Chuck Norris is to notice the music becoming more intense. You might also see ninjas scoping you out from behind trees and on roofs. Death is certain at this point.

CHUCK NORRIS RIDES ON A TANDEM BICYCLE WITH HIS BEARD ON THE SECOND SEAT.

Originally Chuck Norris was going to be hired to play the role of Jack Bauer on the show *24*. The producers changed their minds when they realized the show would last only seventeen minutes.

AREA 51 IS WHERE CHUCK NORRIS KEEPS HIS PETS.

Animators invented CGI to try to do justice to Chuck Norris's beard.

Until Vatican II, the Bible was dedicated to "Chuck Norris's testicles, for making this all possible."

THE ONLY LINE CHUCK NORRIS STANDS IN IS THE LINE OF FIRE.

Chuck Norris once brushed his teeth and invented jazz fusion.

CHUCK NORRIS ONCE PARTOOK IN A PISSING CONTEST OUTSIDE OF A BAR. HIS OPPONENT DROWNED.

Chuck Norris does not know where you live, but he knows where you will die.

There are two types of women: those who want to sleep with Chuck Norris, and those who want to sleep with Chuck Norris again.

CHUCK NORRIS ONCE HAD A HEART ATTACK; HIS HEART LOST.

When Chuck Norris compares apples to oranges, they are equivalent.

Chuck Norris arranged the Bay of Pigs invasion to distract JFK while he slept with Jackie O.

CHUCK NORRIS CAN SPEAK BRAILLE.

Chuck Norris found the goose that laid the golden eggs—then he killed it. Chuck Norris doesn't need handouts.

GRAPPA IS WHAT'S LEFT OVER IN THE CUP WHEN CHUCK NORRIS VISITS THE DENTIST.

Chuck Norris once visited the Virgin Islands. Shortly thereafter, they were renamed The Islands.

Chuck Norris once got in a fight with Lance Armstrong over who had more testicles. Chuck Norris won by three.

Chuck Norris's favorite glove is Steven Tyler.

CHUCK NORRIS DOES NOT LEAVE MESSAGES. CHUCK NORRIS LEAVES WARNINGS.

Chuck Norris once actually made it rain cats and dogs just to take care of a mouse problem.

EVERY TOUR DE FRANCE WINNER HAS DOPED USING CHUCK NORRIS'S BLOOD.

OPRAH LOVES CHUCK NORRIS'S BOOKS.

Chuck Norris will only drive a van if it has the American flag and a bald eagle airbrushed on the side.

Glee was going to do a musical version of a Chuck Norris movie until they found out nobody could sing in the key of awesome.

CHUCK NORRIS OWNS ALL OF THE NO.1 PENCILS.

After he's elected president in 2016, Chuck Norris will replace ObamaCare with ChuckCare. If you get sick, President Norris will let you touch his beard until you feel better.

THE ONLY THING THAT COULD GIVE CHUCK NORRIS INDIGESTION WOULD BE SWALLOWING HIS PRIDE.

When Chuck Norris wants to watch something scary, he pops in the DVD of Barack Obama's inauguration ceremony.

Upset over the reception on his iPhone, Chuck Norris wrote a stern, but polite, letter to Apple. The letter gave Steve Jobs cancer.

CHUCK NORRIS WAS THE FIRST MAN TO SUCCESSFULLY JUMP THE ISLAND OF OAHU IN A FORD TAURUS.

We all know the magic word is "please." As in the sentence, "Please don't kill me." Too bad Chuck Norris doesn't believe in magic.

WATER BOILS FASTER WHEN CHUCK NORRIS WATCHES IT.

When Chuck Norris answers the phone, he just says, "Go." This is not permission for you to begin speaking; it is your cue to start running for your life.

CHUCK NORRIS BEAT AN OCTOPUS AT PING-PONG BEFORE EATING IT WHOLE.

Chuck Norris once played a game of Hearts and shot the moon, killing the entire Apollo space program.

LEBRON JAMES CHOSE MIAMI TO BE NEAR CHUCK NORRIS'S SUMMER HOME.

Intelligent design exists because evolution can't explain how Chuck Norris was born as an ass-kicking machine.

Washington, D.C., gave up on a Chuck Norris monument after five women became pregnant just from looking at his genitals.

CHUCK NORRIS WENT ON MAURY TO PROVE THAT HE'S EVERYONE'S FATHER.

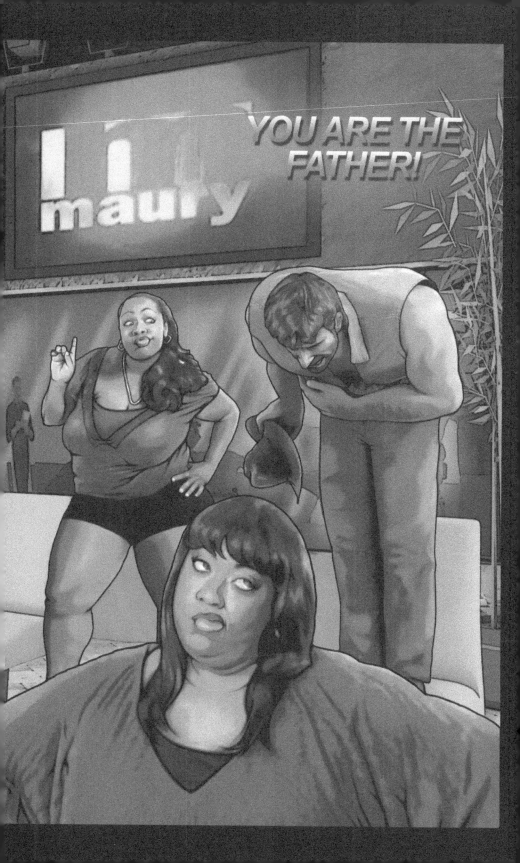

CHUCK NORRIS HAS POCKETS SEWN INTO HIS SKIN.

Switzerland isn't really neutral. They just haven't figured out what side Chuck Norris is on yet.

It's no coincidence that the tattoo on Mike Tyson's face and the sole of Chuck Norris's boots share the same pattern.

CHUCK NORRIS ONCE FELL IN LOVE—THEN THE MIRROR BROKE.

Chuck Norris was once on celebrity *Wheel of Fortune* and was the first to spin. The next twenty-nine minutes of the show consisted of everyone standing around awkwardly, waiting for the wheel to stop.

CHUCK NORRIS SHAVES HIS BALL SACK WITH A JOHN DEERE TRACTOR.

You may have given your girlfriend a diamond necklace for Christmas, but Chuck Norris gave her a pearl one last night.

CHUCK NORRIS DRIVES OPTIMUS PRIME TO WORK.

All bets are off—unless they're all on Chuck Norris.

When Chuck Norris claps with one hand, the sound is deafening.

Inception was written after Christopher Nolan watched Chuck Norris kill ten men in his sleep.

BREWERS OF COORS LIGHT USE CHUCK NORRIS TO TAP THE ROCKIES.

VH1's next reality show will be called *Saddle of Love with Chuck Norris,* where a dozen hormone-crazed women will spend thirteen weeks in a mansion fighting to the death for his pure amusement.

MONA LISA DIDN'T SMILE BEFORE CHUCK NORRIS SPENT A NIGHT IN THE LOUVRE.

Chuck Norris can ripen a melon by squeezing it in his taint.

CHUCK NORRIS DOESN'T NEED TO SIGN UP FOR FACEBOOK TO POKE ANYBODY.

THE RUSSIANS STAGED CHERNOBYL TO COVER UP A CHUCK NORRIS FART.

Chuck Norris once entered a crossword-puzzle contest. He won, and the word "slent" was added to all dictionaries as an acceptable synonym for smell.

As a child, Chuck Norris enjoyed long walks on the beach, particularly Iwo Jima and Normandy.

Chuck Norris once defeated a laser beam in the hundred-meter dash.

Charles Darwin based his "survival of the fittest" theory on Chuck Norris.

In response to the incident at the Fukushima, Japan announced it would replace all of its nuclear power plants with Chuck Norris and a treadmill.

CHUCK NORRIS USES GILLETTE STADIUM TO SHAVE HIS BEARD.

The sixth leading cause of global warming is the steam wafting off Chuck Norris's urine.

The only reason Chuck Norris has never been elected to any government office is because Chuck Norris never runs.

Chuck Norris has to maintain a concealed weapon license in all fifty states in order to legally wear pants.

Each night before he goes to sleep, Chuck Norris calls Dick Cheney for a bedtime story about the invasion of Iraq.

On a road trip when Chuck Norris was eight years old, his father yelled at him, "Don't make me turn this car around!" In response, Chuck punched the backseat so hard, it caused the car to spin a full 180 degrees. He then smirked and said, "Your move, Dad." His father never yelled at him again.

Chuck Norris gets his flu shot, bird shot, and shots of Jägermeister in the same injection.

DR. DREW SPENT 147 DAYS IN REHAB RECOVERING FROM CHUCK NORRIS.

CHUCK NORRIS ROUTINELY PARKS IN FRONT OF FIRE HYDRANTS WHEN HE DRIVES HIS CUSTOM-MADE FIRE TRUCK.

The Library of Congress has archived over thirty thousand different recordings of Chuck Norris reciting the Pledge of Allegiance.

Chuck Norris can prevent forest fires, but he's usually too busy creating them.

Everything Chuck Norris touches does not turn to gold; instead, it grows a beard.

IF CHUCK NORRIS COULD BE ANY TYPE OF TREE, HE WOULD BE TITANIUM.

People say the truth hurts, but it hurts a hell of a lot more when it comes from Chuck Norris.

CHUCK NORRIS AND STEVEN SEAGAL ARE SECRETLY MARRIED. NORRIS WEARS THE PANTS.

When Chuck Norris gives you the finger, he's telling you how many seconds you have left to live.

CHUCK NORRIS INVENTED THE INTERNET SO PEOPLE COULD TALK ABOUT HOW GREAT CHUCK NORRIS IS.

Chuck Norris is so American, he can eat tyranny and shit apple pie.

It is illegal to shout "Fire!" in a crowded movie theater, but if you shout "Chuck Norris is here!" in a crowded movie theater, balloons will fall from the ceiling as you are presented with an oversize check for $25,000.

CHUCK NORRIS AVOIDS AIRPORT SECURITY LINES BY CHECKING HIMSELF IN AS THE PLANE.

In Chuck Norris's fantasy United Nations, the Security Council is run by Ronald Reagan, Ronald McDonald, and Ron Popeil.

THE FENCES AT THE ZOO ARE TO KEEP THE ANIMALS SAFE FROM CHUCK NORRIS.

For some people, one testicle is larger than the other one. For Chuck Norris, each testicle is larger than the other one.

Chuck Norris secretly sleeps with every woman in the world once a month. They bleed for five days as a result.

ALL NINETY-NINE OF JAY-Z'S PROBLEMS ARE CHUCK NORRIS.

Chuck Norris was the first person fired during the 2012 season of *Celebrity Apprentice* for destroying Greece's economy while having sex with Ivanka Trump.

Chuck Norris was the original construction worker in the Village People until he decided to start remodeling the studio while recording "Macho Man."

The only people who would object to Chuck Norris running the New York City schools would be the residents, students, and teachers.

The jihadists are pissed because they can no longer tell their recruits to expect seventy-three virgins in heaven. The best they can now do is seventy-three women who have already had sex with Chuck Norris.

Chuck Norris is currently gathering signatures for a petition so he would be named president of the United States until Barack Obama can provide proof of citizenship.

Chuck Norris learned the hard way that if you feed Wolf Blitzer chocolate, his stomach will explode, killing him instantly.

WHEN CHUCK NORRIS WANTS A SALAD, HE EATS A VEGETARIAN.

Chuck Norris committed a dozen felonies just to be able to meet O. J. Simpson in person.

CHUCK NORRIS CAN SEND FAXES BY STROKING HIS BEARD CLOSE TO A PHONE.

Chuck Norris puts the **"FIST"** in **"PACIFIST."**

SEGA made an arcade game once where you fought Chuck Norris. Every time you put a quarter in, the screen immediately displayed, "You lose." It was SEGA's most popular machine ever.

Chuck Norris beat IBM's Deep Blue computer at chess in three moves. He had only a pawn, a thimble, and a checker.

CHUCK NORRIS'S PENIS HAS ITS OWN ZIP CODE. AT CHRISTMAS TIME IT GETS MORE MAIL THAN SANTA CLAUS.

In the time it took you to read this sentence, Chuck Norris destroyed four thousand acres of rain forest.

If you play Pink Floyd's *The Dark Side of the Moon* and watch *The Wizard of Oz* without sound at the same time, Chuck Norris will beat you senseless for wasting your time.

Chuck Norris will concede that Gary Busey roundly defeated him in a tequila shot-for-shot competition, though Chuck notes that he had spent that morning inventing the printed word.

CHUCK NORRIS ONCE GOT INTO A SCREAMING CONTEST WITH A HORSE.

THE OPPOSITE SIDES OF CHUCK NORRIS ALWAYS ADD UP TO SEVEN.

Chuck Norris once shat in a vase of roses and they went on to live for a thousand years.

CHUCK NORRIS ONCE LIT A FART WHILE CAMPING IN THE SAHARA FOREST.

Chuck Norris hit puberty during the second trimester.

CHUCK NORRIS WAS BAPTIZED WITH NAPALM.

Chuck Norris's Wikipedia entry has been completely fabricated by the Catholic Church.

Chuck Norris has a penis so long that he was the first man to win an Olympic medal for pole-vaulting without the use of a pole.

CHUCK NORRIS'S NIPPLES CAN CAUSE SEVERE TIRE DAMAGE.

Chuck Norris won *America's Got Talent* by standing next to Bruce Springsteen, Stephen King, and Meryl Streep on stage, crossing his arms, and staring intently.

To Chuck Norris, the cup isn't half full or half empty, but always deadly.

BILL GATES LIVES IN CONSTANT FEAR THAT CHUCK NORRIS'S PC WILL CRASH.

The only reason Chuck Norris didn't win an Oscar for his performance in *Sidekicks* is because nobody in their right mind would willingly give Chuck Norris a blunt metal object. That's just suicide.

CHUCK NORRIS CAN KICK A FART BACK INTO AN ASS.

Chuck Norris once brought a man back to life twice and killed him three times because the man had the audacity to die before Chuck Norris was finished killing him.

CHUCK NORRIS HAS ONLY ONE HAND: THE UPPER HAND.

Chuck Norris's calendar goes straight from March 31st to April 2nd; no one fools Chuck Norris.

Chuck Norris visited the Lincoln Memorial and Abe offered him his seat.

Chuck Norris stole your bike.

Chuck Norris has never released some of his movies to the public so that the United States can use them as countermeasures against an attack from an angry Jet Li.

If Chuck Norris were a woman, he wouldn't have a period. He would have an exclamation point.

CHUCK NORRIS ONCE STRUCK LIGHTNING.

Rosa Parks refused to get out of her seat because she was saving it for Chuck Norris.

CHUCK NORRIS OWNS THREE DOGS, TWO HORSES, AND REGIS PHILBIN.

Chuck Norris can spear flying fish out of a raging torrent, with his penis, from inside his car, parked across the street from the river.

Chuck Norris not only walks to the beat of his own drummer, he dances to the spin of his own dreidel and eats to the tune of Bon Jovi.

Chuck Norris owns the other half of the mask from *The Phantom of the Opera*.

GHOSTS ARE ACTUALLY CAUSED BY CHUCK NORRIS KILLING PEOPLE FASTER THAN DEATH CAN PROCESS THEM.

Chuck Norris never loses a game of Clue, despite the fact everyone knows he's the murderer and used his foot to do it.

Someone once bet Chuck Norris he couldn't shit on the ceiling. Michelangelo still owes him ten bucks.

AS A CHILD, CHUCK NORRIS PLAYED HUNGRY HUNGRY HIPPOS WITH REAL HIPPOS.

Objects in Chuck Norris's rearview mirror appear at their correct distances.

WHEN CHUCK NORRIS HAD SURGERY, THE ANESTHESIA WAS APPLIED TO THE DOCTORS.

Before he goes onstage, Chuck Norris breaks someone's leg to give himself good luck.

Chuck Norris is the only Olympic diver to ever get a gold medal for performing a half somersault with five twists after jumping off his own boner.

THE ONLY TIME CHUCK NORRIS HAS EVER BEEN WRONG IS THE TIME HE THOUGHT HE HAD MADE A MISTAKE.

Chuck Norris taught a school of fish how to kill members of Greenpeace.

CHUCK NORRIS IS SO CONSERVATIVE THAT HE WON'T EVEN USE HIS LEFT HAND.

Chuck Norris has three human centipedes and one human millipede on back order.

Chuck Norris's childhood Halloween stories were adapted to film as *Saw I, II,* and *III*.

CHUCK NORRIS'S SPERM BANK DEPOSITS GAIN INTEREST.

The difference between Chuck Norris and Listerine is that Chuck Norris fights bad breath and germs with his fists.

CHUCK NORRIS ONCE HAD AN ERECTION WHILE LYING FACE DOWN, AND STRUCK OIL.

It is said that the U.S. Army does not have enough bullets to kill the solders of the Chinese Army in the event of an invasion. Lucky for us, Chuck Norris's foot doesn't need ammo.

When Chuck was asked why he never goes to the bathroom, he replied, "What happens in Chuck Norris stays in Chuck Norris."

CHUCK NORRIS CLEANS THE WAX OUT OF HIS EARS WITH A SHOTGUN.

For a small fee, Chuck Norris will kill your family pet and then blame it on the Jews.

When he was a seven-year-old, Chuck Norris's mom once told him to go and dig to China. He left and returned three weeks later with a second-degree black belt in Eagle Claw Kung Fu.

WHEN CHUCK NORRIS PLAYS GOLF, THEY HAVE TO PUT THE HOLE ON THE MOON.

CHUCK NORRIS'S BEARD
IS SPACE'S FINAL FRONTIER.

Chuck Norris is like corn. No matter how much shit he is in he still comes out in one piece.

CHUCK NORRIS BUILT THE PANAMA CANAL WITH ONE HAND.

CHUCK NORRIS'S DRIVER'S LICENSE PHOTO LOOKS AMAZING.

Chuck Norris was on an episode of *Press Your Luck*. When it was Chuck Norris's turn, he said, "C'mon, no Whammies." No one has since seen another Whammy, nor another episode of *Press Your Luck*.

CHUCK NORRIS ONCE RAN FOR SENATE IN TEXAS AND WON BOTH SEATS.

Chuck Norris can eat enough burritos from Chipotle in a single sitting to fill four Olympic-size diving pools.

CHUCK NORRIS'S GOLF CLUBS ARE CRAFTED FROM THE BONES OF MASTODONS.

CHUCK NORRIS DOES NOT WEAR A CUP. HE WEARS A BARREL.

Mr. T once defeated Chuck Norris in a game of tic-tac-toe. In retaliation, Chuck Norris invented racism.

The one-dollar bill originally had Chuck Norris on it, but the beard kept getting caught in vending machines.

Chuck Norris was born with two umbilical cords, one red and one blue. The bomb squad cut the wrong one.

WHEN CHUCK NORRIS CUTS IN LINE, THE LINE BLEEDS.

Chuck Norris is a vegetarian—he does not eat animals until he first puts them into a vegetative state.

Chuck Norris was given the key to the city of Bozeman, Montana, after hijacking a plane full of tourists and landing it there.

CHUCK NORRIS WON THE CRUSADES BY T.K.O.

Chuck Norris is planning to produce *Ocean's Fourteen,* a story about how he and thirteen partners plan to rob you of eighty-five minutes and $11.

CHUCK NORRIS IS THE CURRENT REIGNING WORLD CHAMPION OF YU-GI-OH! CARDS.

Chuck Norris has been known to commandeer entire ocean liners with only determination and a harpoon gun.

Chuck Norris went on *Nickelodeon GUTS* and won all the events without any bungee cords. Then he had sex with Mo on top of the Aggro Crag.

Chuck Norris has Braille on his boots so that even blind people will know what's coming.

Every night before going to sleep, the bogeyman checks under his bed for Chuck Norris.

WHEN CHUCK NORRIS BREAKS WIND, IT STAYS BROKEN.

Sometimes, while setting, the sun will linger just a few more minutes on the horizon to get one last look at Chuck Norris.

Chuck Norris ate a box of Alpha-Bits cereal and shat out the entire works of Edgar Allan Poe.

CHUCK NORRIS'S MILD-MANNERED ALTER EGO IS SUPERMAN.

Chuck Norris can kill you in more ways than you know how to die.

CHUCK NORRIS HAS HAD HIS CAKE AND HAS EATEN IT, AND NOW HE WANTS YOURS.

When Chuck Norris eats airplane food, it tastes good.

THE U.S. FOREST SERVICE MAINTAINS ALL OF CHUCK NORRIS'S HAIR.

Chuck Norris once squeezed an M&M so hard that it turned into a Skittle.

Piñatas were made in an attempt to get Chuck Norris to stop kicking the people of Mexico. Sadly, this backfired, as all it has resulted in is Chuck Norris looking for candy after he kicks his victims.

LOVE MEANS CHUCK NORRIS NEVER HAS TO SAY HE'S SORRY.

When Superman squeezes a lump of coal, he creates a diamond. When Chuck Norris squeezes a lump of coal, he creates an African child to work in his diamond mines.

One time, Chuck Norris's son went missing. He was found in Chuck Norris's beard two months later.

When Chuck Norris deletes files from his computer, he doesn't send them to the Recycle Bin. **HE SENDS THEM TO HELL.**

As a child, when Chuck Norris came home from trick-or-treating on Halloween, he returned with a bag full of candy, a bag full of miniature liquor bottles, an Irish Setter, and two underage prostitutes carrying more of his candy.

CHUCK NORRIS HAS BEEN KNOWN TO FRY BACON IN THE NUDE. KEVIN BACON, THAT IS.

WHEN CHUCK NORRIS IS TRYING TO CUT WEIGHT FOR AN MMA FIGHT HE SWITCHES TO DRINKING UNLEADED GASOLINE.

In the comments section of Chuck Norris's first-grade report card, it said, "What Mr. Norris lacks in social skills he makes up for in the bedroom."

The book *The Worst-Case Scenario Survival Handbook* discusses ways to run from many deadly animals. The page entitled "Running from Chuck Norris" simply says, "Good luck."

CHUCK NORRIS ONCE PLAYED DUCK DUCK GOOSE WITH A GROUP OF KINDERGARTENERS. ONLY ONE KID MADE IT TO FIRST GRADE.

After running out of ammo, Chuck Norris stood in the line of fire, took three shots to the chest, and used them to reload.

ONCE, A COBRA BIT CHUCK NORRIS'S LEG. AFTER FIVE DAYS OF EXCRUCIATING PAIN, THE COBRA DIED.

Chuck Norris never loses at rock-paper-scissors because he never plays rock-paper-scissors. He plays rock-paper-scissors-roundhouse kick. Chuck Norris never loses at rock-paper-scissors-roundhouse kick.

DUE TO THE FAVORABLE EXCHANGE RATE, A CHUCK NORRIS IN THE HAND IS WORTH ABOUT 3.5 IN THE BUSH.

In a recent press conference, Chuck Norris confirmed rumors that he was going to allow Arnold Schwarzenegger to enter his urethra so that he could be reborn at a later date and be eligible for the United States presidency.

WHEN CHUCK NORRIS FINISHES A MEAL, THE PLATE IS CLEANER THAN IT WAS BEFORE THE FOOD WAS PUT ON IT.

Chuck Norris represents the East Side, but has the West Side rappers under his control, too.

Give MacGyver a toothpick and a pocketknife and he'll escape from handcuffs. Give Chuck Norris the same tools and he'll win a war, climb Mount Everest, and build a new mansion while carrying around a pocketknife and a toothpick.

CHUCK NORRIS'S REAL NAME IS SWITCHBLADE KILLINGSWORTH. HE CHANGED IT TO CHUCK NORRIS BECAUSE IT SOUNDED TOUGHER.

Chuck Norris once thought he was stuck between a rock and a hard place. He quickly realized he was standing between two mirrors.

CHUCK NORRIS HAS "MADE IN U.S.A." TATTOOED ON HIS TAINT.

Chuck Norris once put on a pair of roller skates and showed up at a quarry looking for a job. He is now the most powerful dump truck known to man.

CHUCK NORRIS CAN STARE YOU DOWN WITH HIS BACK TURNED.

Chuck Norris has been scientifically proven to be cheaper and more effective at preventing premature aging than the world's leading beauty products. For just twenty dollars, Chuck Norris will agree to show up unannounced at your house at some point just before your thirtieth birthday and kill you.

CHUCK NORRIS HAS A BOY SCOUT MERIT BADGE IN DONKEY PUNCHING.

Economists closely monitor sales of Chuck Norris movies to determine the health of the global economy.

The eternal conundrum "what happens when an unstoppable force meets an immovable object" was finally solved when Chuck Norris punched himself in the face.

CHUCK NORRIS DEEPLY ADMIRES AND RESPECTS THE MOUNTAIN GOAT.

"Don't Ask, Don't Tell" was originally standard military shorthand for "If the enemies don't ask, don't tell them Chuck Norris is here."

As a kid, Chuck Norris would always get picked last for the soccer team because at the first opportunity he would roundhouse kick the ball into the sun.

Chuck Norris's face has only two expressions, **ONE OF WHICH HAS NEVER BEEN SEEN.**

Chuck Norris left his first and only Iron and Wine concert very disappointed because there was no smelting or grapes.

Chuck Norris is the only person on the planet who can kick you in the back of the face.

CHUCK NORRIS IS ALWAYS ON TOP DURING SEX BECAUSE CHUCK NORRIS NEVER FUCKS UP.

Never use the phrase "eat my heart out" around Chuck Norris. He will.

THIRTY PERCENT OF THE TIME, CHUCK NORRIS'S FAVORITE PIE IS CHART.

Chuck Norris once broke a mirror on a black cat under a ladder on Friday the thirteenth. He won the lottery later that day.

Chuck Norris slept through 9/11. His bedroom was on the seventy-third floor.

THE ONLY MATCH FOR CHUCK NORRIS IS THE ONE HE BURNS YOU WITH.

CHUCK NORRIS BUILDS ALL THE HOME DEPOTS WITH HIS BARE HANDS.

The term "heartburn" was invented when Chuck Norris roundhouse kicked a man in the chest and his heart caught fire.

CHUCK NORRIS PROTECTS RON PAUL'S GOLD COINS.

Man once believed that Chuck Norris revolved around the earth; today we know the opposite to be true, and the terrible price those fools paid for their ignorance.

PICTURES OF CHUCK NORRIS ARE WORTH TWO THOUSAND WORDS.

When Chuck Norris looks in a mirror, the mirror shatters, because not even glass is stupid enough to get in between Chuck Norris and Chuck Norris.

CHURCH FATHERS EDITED OUT THE PART OF THE GOSPEL WHERE CHUCK NORRIS RAPPELLED INTO THE LAST SUPPER, KARATE-CHOPPED THE TABLE, AND TEA-BAGGED JUDAS.

Death once had a near–Chuck Norris experience.

CHUCK NORRIS DOESN'T SLEEP.
HE WAITS.

A man once told Chuck Norris there was no wrong way to eat a Reese's. Chuck Norris promptly showed him that there was by killing the man's wife with it.

Chuck Norris hates Native Americans, even though he's part Native American himself. Chuck Norris also hates irony.

RATHER THAN TAKE SHOWERS, CHUCK NORRIS RIDES A NINE-FOOT GRIZZLY BEAR THROUGH A CAR WASH.

The famous video footage of Sasquatch is actually Chuck Norris returning to his woodland home.

HELEN KELLER'S FAVORITE COLOR IS CHUCK NORRIS.

Chuck Norris feels no attraction to men or women, only to hyperintelligent shades of blue.

CHUCK NORRIS DOESN'T LAUGH;
HE SUES.

Chuck Norris accidentally created Optimus Prime while trying to come up with a prototype for the Total Gym.

IF YOU HAVE FIVE DOLLARS AND CHUCK NORRIS HAS FIVE DOLLARS, CHUCK NORRIS HAS MORE MONEY THAN YOU.

Frustrated with poor reception, Chuck Norris replaced his car radio with a trailer and the Mormon Tabernacle Choir.

Chuck Norris won't allow his children to be taught evolution at school. This wouldn't be a big deal, but he fathered 70 percent of the people in the southern United States.

CHUCK NORRIS IS THE SI UNIT OF FEAR.

Chuck Norris has a prehensile tail that he has trained himself to knife fight with.

Chuck Norris once walked a mile in shoes made out of another man.

It's believed that Moses parted the Red Sea, but the truth is that Chuck Norris was just walking over from the other side at the same time.

CHUCK NORRIS IS NEITHER PRO-CHOICE NOR PRO-LIFE. HE IS PRO-DEATH.

When a drop of Chuck Norris's sweat hits the ground, it transforms into a miniature bald eagle and flies off in the direction of Mount Rushmore.

In addition to wanting to be president of Texas, Chuck Norris plans to become deputy mayor of Indianapolis, the Armenian representative to the U.N., fire marshal of Tokyo, and moon senator of District Alpha-38, Sea of Tranquility.

CHUCK NORRIS'S BEARD IS ON THE NO-FLY LIST.

CHUCK NORRIS IS THE REASON WHY CAP'N CRUNCH WAS TURNED DOWN FOR HIS PROMOTION TO ADMIRAL.

Chuck Norris broke the record for the highest cannonball when he jumped from the International Space Station into the Indian Ocean.

THE ONLY TYPE OF FEVER CHUCK NORRIS EVER GETS IS DISCO FEVER.

Chuck Norris keeps his balls in a holster and his dick in a guitar case.

Chuck Norris's turds float so well that one of them won the gold medal in the two-hundred-meter backstroke at the 1984 Olympics.

THE MOVIE *CONGO* WAS FILMED ENTIRELY IN CHUCK NORRIS'S BACK HAIR.

THE CHINESE IDEOGRAM FOR "CHUCK NORRIS" DEPICTS THE HEAVEN ABOVE, GROWING A BEARD.

God once made a rock so big that not even He could lift it, thus answering the legendary philosophical question. Chuck Norris not only lifted this rock, but also karate chopped it so hard that it fragmented and formed the progressive rock group Yes.

Chuck Norris saved President Bush from choking on a pretzel by roundhouse kicking him in the throat. Chuck had no idea he was choking.

Angelo Vildasol

WHEN CHUCK NORRIS FIGHTS IN COURT, THE STENOGRAPHER IS ALWAYS THE FIRST TO GO.

When Chuck Norris was offered a golden parachute, he turned it down because everybody knows that when dropped from any height, Chuck Norris will always land on his hands and feet without harm.

Chuck Norris can only donate his left kidney because the right one was replaced with a hand grenade in 1973.

CHUCK NORRIS INVENTED THE BIG BANG THEORY AFTER FUCKING ALBERT EINSTEIN'S WIFE.

The only way to tickle Chuck Norris is to douse him in kerosene and light him on fire with a welding torch.

Chuck Norris's toenail clippings are harvested monthly and are the primary ingredient in asphalt.

A freak accident involving Chuck Norris and a severe thunderstorm turned an ordinary Total Gym into Richard Dean Anderson, star of TV series *MacGyver*. Scholars around the world maintain that this is the only known case of irony that is both situational and dramatic.

Chuck Norris commissioned the construction of a giant claw cracker and used it to eat Iron Man.

ANY FRIDAY WHEN CHUCK NORRIS WALKS INTO A STORE EXPECTING A DEAL IS CONSIDERED BLACK FRIDAY.

Chuck Norris's circadian rhythm is an exact match to the guitar solo in "Free Bird."

EVERY EXIT IN CHUCK NORRIS'S OFFICE IS AN EMERGENCY EXIT.

Chuck Norris is the only person to have won a uranium medal in the Olympics.

EVERY TIME CHUCK NORRIS LEAVES A ROOM, THE SONG "MY HERO" STARTS PLAYING OUT OF NOWHERE.

Chuck Norris has won a number of Emmys but refuses to accept the awards until the statuette grows a beard.

You know Chuck Norris isn't a zombie because he likes eggs whole and raw and likes brains scrambled and fluffy and not the other way around.

Chuck Norris has set aside next summer to "take back the Jersey Shore."

The only reason Optimus Prime came back at the end of *Transformers 2* was because Chuck Norris had some replacement parts in his garage.

CHUCK NORRIS CAN KILL A MAN IN A RAP BATTLE.

Chuck Norris can play the bongo drums with his hands behind his back. He accomplishes this by leaning over them really close and flexing his pecs. The sweet rhythms he produces are the most potent form of aphrodisiac known to man.

Chuck Norris will never get rid of his Milli Vanilli albums because Chuck Norris never takes out the trash.

Chuck Norris coined the phrase "I could eat a horse" after he ate the last unicorn in existence.

Some people get wasted with rounds of shots; Chuck Norris gets wasted with rounds of shotguns.

CHUCK NORRIS BUILT A WIND FARM TO POWER HIS CHAIN OF GAS STATIONS.

Actuaries worldwide agree that the least likely event to ever occur on Earth is Chuck Norris becoming really good friends with Tracy Morgan.

ALL OF THE ACTIONS PERFORMED BY A CHUCK NORRIS ACTION FIGURE ARE HATE CRIMES.

CHUCK NORRIS WANTS TO ALLOW PRAYER IN SCHOOL, BUT ONLY PRAYERS TO HIM.

The English rock band Muse was funded by Chuck Norris's desire for something to listen to while riding horses on fire during his annual trip across the galaxy to Alpha Centauri.

Chuck Norris won a race against a man up eight flights of stairs to a rooftop, across an alley, to a collapsing building, into a waiting sports car driven by a beautiful woman because he was Chuck Norris and the man racing him had no arms or legs.

CHUCK NORRIS HAS A TATTOO ABOVE HIS PELVIS THAT READS, "TASTES GREAT, MORE FILLING!"

CHUCK NORRIS HAS ACTUALLY
LIFTED TEXAS BY ITS PANHANDLE.

Many people say that Chuck Norris eats babies. This is not true. Babies just want to be in Chuck Norris's stomach.

In 1979, Chuck Norris became the first black man to win the New York City Marathon.

CHUCK NORRIS ATE THE LAST PIECE OF PIZZA. WHAT ARE YOU GONNA DO ABOUT IT?

If you disagree with Chuck Norris, he'll karate chop you into a bajillion pieces. He is aware that this is not a number, but if you call him on it, he'll roundhouse kick you into a quabillion.

CHUCK NORRIS CAN BEAT A BRICK WALL IN TENNIS.

Chuck Norris has won both the annual camel fighting and beauty pageants in Selçuk, Turkey, for seven years in a row.

THERE ARE OVER SIX HUNDRED MILES OF BLACK BELTS INSIDE CHUCK NORRIS'S HOME.

CHUCK NORRIS DRIVES AN ICE CREAM TRUCK COVERED IN HUMAN SKULLS.

A midget, a rabbi, and a horse all walk into a bar. Ah, fuck it. Chuck Norris roundhouse kicked all their asses.

Chuck Norris doesn't have to cut his grass; he just stands on his porch and dares it to grow.

Chuck Norris is diversifying into pharmaceuticals. He will soon be releasing two new products. The first is a medication to help control hemorrhoids. It is called "Preparation—Chuck's Foot." The other product is used to control erectile dysfunction. It is called "Chuck's Other Foot."

THE CREDIT CRUNCH IS PART OF CHUCK NORRIS'S MORNING WORKOUT.

If you watch *Walker, Texas Ranger* closely, you'll notice that Chuck Norris uses violence only as a last resort, or when the world goes in slow motion.

Chuck Norris has secretly kept a speech for an Oscar® win for the last twenty-five years. It starts, "I can't fucking believe this either, but . . ."

Chuck likes his meat so rare that **HE ONLY EATS UNICORNS.**

Chuck Norris rescued thirteen infants from Charity Hospital following the devastation of Hurricane Katrina. He did not have a boat. He has not returned the babies.

THE ONLY MERCY CHUCK NORRIS KNOWS IS MERCY JOHNSON OF TOPEKA, KANSAS, BECAUSE HE TOOK HER VIRGINITY SEVEN TIMES.

Chuck Norris's sperm are approximately the size of red salmon. When Chuck's sperm mature, they travel up a river to be caught and eaten by thirsty Japanese girls.

CHUCK NORRIS REPACKAGES HIS USED PAPER TOWEL ROLLS AS 150-IN-1 ULTIMATE ASSASSIN TOOLS.

If you paint one painting, you're not a painter. But Chuck Norris baked one cake, and he currently holds the title of World's Best Baker.

CHUCK NORRIS IS A MAN'S MAN'S MAN.

Chuck Norris eats beef jerky and shits gunpowder. Then he uses that gunpowder to make a bullet, which he uses to kill a cow and make more beef jerky. Some people refer to this as the "Circle of Life."

In the game of life, Chuck Norris has the only retired jersey.

Chuck Norris has no pancreas. He instead has a retroperitoneal waffle iron that excretes a pancreatic juice made of liquid vengeance.

CHUCK NORRIS GOT IN TOUCH WITH HIS FEMININE SIDE, AND PROMPTLY GOT HER PREGNANT.

The MLB team is called the Texas Rangers only because calling themselves the Texas Walkers seemed like bad mojo for the pitchers.

CHUCK NORRIS WAS ACTUALLY DR. MARTIN LUTHER KING, JR.'S DREAM.

Chuck Norris retired from competitive tap-dancing after being mistaken by authorities as the epicenter of the 1989 Loma Prieta earthquake.

CHUCK NORRIS'S PENIS HAS CONDUCTED OVER A DOZEN SYMPHONY ORCHESTRAS.

A head-butt from Chuck Norris delivers the same force as a thirty-mile-per-hour car crash and the same surprise as triplets.

CHUCK NORRIS ONCE SAVED A
BUSLOAD OF CHILDREN FROM
CERTAIN PERIL BY WATCHING THEM
BURN TO CERTAIN DEATH.

Chuck Norris keeps hundreds of lobbyists employed due to his sheer desire to have Congress officially rename global warming "Bieber Fever."

CHUCK NORRIS CAN BE TRIGGERED TO KILL JUST BY WATCHING *HUCKABEE*.

Chuck Norris owns the largest collection of commemorative tectonic plates.

Chuck Norris is just like Jesus, except Chuck Norris won't die for your sins. Instead, you'll die for his.

Chuck Norris once decided to make a vibrator that would simulate the size and power of his actual penis. The result was a baseball bat wrapped in barbed wire and bolted to a jackhammer.

CHUCK NORRIS OFTEN ASKS PEOPLE TO PULL HIS FINGER. WHEN THEY DO, HE ROUNDHOUSES THEM IN THE ABDOMEN. THEN HE FARTS.

Back in the '80s, Chuck Norris had a swimming pool installed in his house in the shape of his beard and then filled it with the tears of his enemies.

Bruce Lee never died. The true cause of his disappearance is that he asked Chuck Norris to teach him how to perform a roundhouse kick. Being good friends, Chuck Norris promised to teach him, but only after Bruce Lee embarked on an epic journey of the spirit that is still taking place entirely within Chuck Norris's beard.

KING KONG ONCE CHALLENGED GODZILLA TO AN ARM-WRESTLING MATCH. CHUCK NORRIS WON.

Chuck Norris keeps trying to donate sperm, but the receptionist keeps getting pregnant.

CHUCK NORRIS DOES NOT OPEN DOORS FOR HIS DATE. HE ROUNDHOUSE KICKS THEM DOWN. HER, TOO.

Chuck Norris can rub any *Family Guy* DVD on his beard and instantly make it funny again the next time you watch it.

THERE IS NOTHING TO FEAR BUT FEAR ITSELF, AND FEAR ITSELF FEARS CHUCK NORRIS.

King George VI hired Lionel Logue as a speaking coach because Chuck Norris only taught him how to negotiate for a good deal on an F-150.

THE WORD "FUCK" IS IN FACT A PORTMANTEAU OF "FOOT OF CHUCK."

If at the exact same moment, the same person was pitied by Mr. T and roundhouse kicked by Chuck Norris, the universe would implode.

Most children remember bringing an apple to school for the teacher. Chuck Norris brought the teacher's ex-husband's heart in a plastic baggie.

NOT ONLY IS HE PART OF THE MILE HIGH CLUB, CHUCK NORRIS IS ALSO IN THE MILE LONG CLUB AND THE MILE WIDE CLUB.

Tim Tebow might play backup quarterback for the Jets, but Chuck Norris was in a one-man remake of *West Side Story* where he played *all* of the Jets.

CHUCK NORRIS ONCE CLIMBED MOUNT EVEREST BY ACCIDENT.

Chuck Norris hates ballerinas because they twirl all day and not a single person gets roundhouse kicked in the face.

Chuck Norris once roundhouse kicked a waitress because his steak didn't have a beard.

Chuck Norris uses ribbed condoms inside out, so he gets the pleasure.

CHUCK NORRIS IS SO GOOD HE'LL SHIT YOUR PANTS FOR YOU.

Chuck Norris does not have AIDS but he gives it to people anyway.

ALL OF CHUCK NORRIS'S FORMAL ATTIRE IS MADE OF DENIM.

The last time Chuck Norris woke up after a night of binge drinking, he found himself negotiating the terms of the Louisiana Purchase.

IF CHUCK NORRIS TAKES OUT A LOAN, THE ONLY COLLATERAL HE PROVIDES IS COLLATERAL DAMAGE.

Chuck Norris's favorite pickup line is made of one-eighth-inch steel cable, has a tensile strength of 4,700 pounds, and is tied at one end to a Ford Bronco.

Chuck Norris inadvertently discovered cold fusion when he poured two beers into a single glass.

CHUCK NORRIS CAN MAKE
A HORSE CRY JUST
BY DROPPING HIS PANTS.

The postman always rings twice and leaves you with mail; Chuck Norris usually rings twice and leaves your fridge devoid of meat products.

CHUCK NORRIS'S CREDIT CARD EARNS MILES WITH EVERY PILOT HE SHOOTS DOWN.

If you look in a mirror and say "Chuck Norris" three times, he will appear and kill your entire family, but at least you get to see Chuck Norris.

Chuck Norris keeps Four Loko on tap. **IN HIS TRUCK.**

Chuck Norris can get a girl's number while landing a 747, extinguishing a four-alarm fire, and knocking out her boyfriend, all at the same time.

Law & Order is a series of weekly hour-long reenactments of Chuck Norris's legendary career as the NYPD's finest police car.

Upon hearing that his good friend, Lance Armstrong, lost his testicles to cancer, Chuck Norris donated one of his to Lance. With just one of Chuck's nuts, Lance was able to win the Tour de France seven times. By the way, Chuck still has two testicles; either he was able to produce a new one simply by flexing, or he had three to begin with. No one knows for sure.

CHUCK NORRIS HAS WON EVERY CONTEST THAT HE'S ENTERED. EVEN MISS NUDE WISCONSIN.

Motor Trend's award for best hybrid of 2010 was given to Chuck Norris for completing a triathlon.

The *Walker, Texas Ranger* video game was discontinued after Chuck Norris's character came out of the TV and killed three teenagers.

CHUCK NORRIS RUNS A BACK-ALLEY RADIOLOGY CLINIC.

Chuck Norris always has a smirk on his face when he watches the show *I Didn't Know I Was Pregnant.*

Chuck Norris runs the most popular shadow puppet government in sub-Saharan Africa.

Between 2004 and 2008, Chuck Norris trained
seventeen velociraptors to seek out and kill
democrats.

CHUCK NORRIS'S DREAM WOMAN IS A CINDERBLOCK WITH A VAGINA, SURROUNDED BY ANGRY BEES.

When Chuck Norris threw a frat party in college, it was
out of a third-floor plateglass window.

IF CHUCK NORRIS HAD A DOLLAR FOR EVERY TIME HE HEARD "I DIDN'T KNOW YOU COULD FIT THAT IN THERE," HE WOULD HAVE $38,982.

The concept of the smoke monster in *Lost* was based
on an old home movie of Chuck Norris chasing
communists through jungle brush.

Chuck Norris won a lifetime achievement award from the American Ventriloquists Association for turning Mike Huckabee into his personal hand puppet for the entire 2008 presidential campaign.

Michael Jackson was taking all of those anti-anxiety medications because he borrowed a pair of boots from Chuck Norris and never returned them.

IN EXCHANGE FOR TUTORING HIS SON IN MATH, CHUCK NORRIS TAUGHT JEREMY LIN HOW TO PLAY BASKETBALL.

Anything with Chuck Norris's signature on it is considered legal tender in Belgium.

Rather than drink a cup of coffee every morning, Chuck Norris pours the whole pot on his genitals.

CHUCK NORRIS EATS THREE SQUARE MEALS A DAY. HIS BEARD EATS SEVEN.

Chuck Norris's beard is pure matter, and his chest hair is pure antimatter. **IF THE TWO EVER MEET, THE UNIVERSE WILL EXPLODE.**

When Chuck Norris was on Noah's ark, the dragons scuffed his snakeskin boots. That was all it took.

Like many celebrities, Chuck Norris adopts African babies. Except he does it as part of his side project, the World's Biggest Ball of African Babies.

The greatest trick the devil ever pulled was convincing Chuck Norris to give him the name and number for his accountant.

THERE'S NO "I" IN TEAM, BUT THERE IS ONE IN CHUCK NORRIS. IT'S A FAIRLY EASY NAME TO SPELL REALLY.

Chuck Norris will soon be starting a new website called Chuckslist where you can sell anything you want to Chuck Norris in exchange for shares of News Corporation.

When Chuck Norris roundhouse kicks you, he tears a hole in the fabric of space and time, which sucks you into a parallel universe filled with Chuck Norrises, all waiting to roundhouse kick you.

CHUCK NORRIS FIRED CONRAD MURRAY FOR HIS TASTE IN WOMEN.

In the 2008 Summer Olympics, Michael Phelps won eight gold medals. Shortly thereafter, Chuck Norris won eight gold medals in the parking lot of the Beijing National Aquatics Center. Chuck Norris is still trying to get Scaring the Shit Out of Michael Phelps recognized as an official Olympic event.

CHUCK NORRIS DOESN'T NEED A WEAPON. HE *IS* ONE.

Whenever Chuck Norris sees a Best Buy, he burns it to the ground, because he firmly believes that a Total Gym for three easy payments of $19.99 is the best buy you'll ever find.

CHUCK NORRIS SHOPS FOR CARS BASED ON THEIR SPEED RELATIVE TO THE BATMOBILE.

Justin Bieber's entire head of hair was grown from a single strand of Chuck Norris's pubes.

Chuck Norris beat *Final Fantasy XIII* on an Atari 2600.

**Chuck Norris's erection
is visible from space.**

CHUCK NORRIS HAS DENIM GENES.

Chuck Norris used the majority of the money he made for *Missing in Action 2* to have the inside of his wife's vagina lined with denim.

CHUCK NORRIS HAS HAD SEX ON EVERY TOTAL GYM THAT HAS BEEN SOLD IN THE MIDWEST.

Chuck Norris's first girlfriend gave him the nickname "7-11" because he was seven inches limp and eleven hard. They broke up when he was eight.

CHUCK NORRIS'S FAVORITE DISEASE IS PREGNANCY.

Chuck Norris was to appear in the *Street Fighter II* video game, but was removed by programmers because every button caused him to do a roundhouse kick. When asked about this "glitch," Norris replied, "That's no glitch."

Chuck Norris's first uncredited role in a movie was as the rabbit in *Monty Python and the Holy Grail*.

CHUCK NORRIS CAN MATHEMATICALLY MAKE TWO WRONGS EQUAL A RIGHT.

On Ash Wednesday, Chuck Norris's priest says, "Remember, Chuck Norris, that you are awesome."

CHUCK NORRIS COMMITS ARMED ROBBERY WITH OTHER PEOPLE'S ARMS.

Chuck Norris surprisingly came out in favor of gay marriage because it would allow his testicles to be wed.

CHUCK NORRIS OWNS ENOUGH BLACK BELTS TO CIRCLE THE EARTH ELEVEN TIMES.

In the 2010 elections, Chuck Norris literally won the House back for Republicans room by room, starting in the lobby.

CHUCK NORRIS EATS DINOSAUR BONES AND CRAPS OUT HIGH-GRADE PETROLEUM.

Chuck Norris has routinely lit his underwear on fire on board transcontinental flights for years without any problems.

IN 2010, THIRTY-THREE CHILEAN MINERS LOST A BET TO CHUCK NORRIS THAT THEY COULDN'T AFFORD TO PAY.

Chuck Norris celebrates the Fourth of July every year by proclaiming his own independence and drinking an ice-cold beer from the skull of King George III.

Should you ever come across Chuck Norris in the woods, remember that he is probably just as afraid as you aren't.

CHUCK NORRIS WON A TONY AWARD FOR HAILING A CAB ON BROADWAY.

Chuck Norris can take over the world **FASTER THAN A NEW COLDPLAY ALBUM.**

Chuck Norris can build a fleet of locomotives in the time between *The Early Show* and *The Late Show*.

CHUCK NORRIS CAN CUT THROUGH A KNIFE WITH A STICK OF BUTTER.

Chuck Norris ate mathematician Pierre de Fermat and crapped out a proof to his Last Theorem. (Chuck's colon is Lucasian Professor of Mathematics at Cambridge University.)

CHUCK NORRIS AND DIRK BENEDICT ARE THE ONLY SURVIVING FOUNDERS OF THE BEST NAMES OF THE EIGHTIES CLUB.

When *Walker, Texas Ranger* aired for the first time in high definition, 300,000 women in the Midwest had simultaneous orgasms.

The term "nunchuck" was coined after Chuck Norris used a pair of Catholic nuns as weapons to mercilessly beat an angry mob to death. Chuck makes weapons from his surroundings.

EVERY WALL IN CHUCK NORRIS'S HOUSE IS A MIRROR BECAUSE CHUCK NORRIS MUST ALWAYS BE SURROUNDED BY BEAUTY.

Whenever Chuck Norris successfully completes a vicious roundhouse kick to the face he sings to himself "This Is How We Do It" by Montell Jordan.

Jesus's birthday isn't December twenty-fifth, but Chuck Norris once sent him a birthday card on that day. Jesus was too scared to tell Chuck the truth, and that's why we celebrate Christmas.

Everyone has a skeleton in their closet. Chuck Norris has 7,483.

EVERY YEAR CHUCK NORRIS ASKS HIS DOCTOR TO VACCINATE HIM FOR H1N1, TETANUS, AND THE *SEINFELD* CURSE.

At any U.S. airport security checkpoint, you can ask a TSA agent to bring you to a separate security screening where Chuck Norris looks you in the eyes and dares you to walk past him with anything illegal.

Chuck Norris once made David Copperfield disappear by staring at him and telling him to get the fuck off his lawn.

CHUCK NORRIS CAN BOIL WATER IN NINETY SECONDS WITH HIS MICROWAVE-EMITTING CORNEAS.

Chuck Norris banged Christie Brinkley, and nine months later she gave birth to the Total Gym.

Scientists have attempted to calculate the statistical possibility of anyone beating Chuck Norris. The sheer impossibility of this task has caused many of the scientists to develop severe foot-shaped bruising to the face.

CHUCK NORRIS TAUGHT THE STIG HOW TO DRIVE.

Chuck Norris once convinced a polar bear that global warming doesn't exist.

The American Museum of Natural History abandoned plans for an exhibit called "The Conquests of Chuck Norris" when they realized Chuck Norris has never left anything standing for them to display.

DRIVERS SLOW DOWN ON THE HIGHWAY NEAR ACCIDENTS TO TRY TO SEE IF CHUCK NORRIS IS NEARBY.

Werner Heisenberg discovered his uncertainty principle when he realized it was impossible to determine both where Chuck Norris's fist was and how fast it was moving at the same time.

ON HUMID DAYS,
CHUCK NORRIS'S BEARD
ALSO DOUBLES AS A FLY ZAPPER.

In 1929, the United States Mint announced Chuck Norris would be featured on the dime. They quickly changed it back to the head of Mercury after the Chuck Norris dime became worth $4,000, plunging America into the Great Depression.

It is said you can't know someone until you walk a mile in their shoes. This means no one will ever know Chuck Norris because he'd kill you if you touched his shoes.

CHUCK NORRIS WILL EAT
YOUR SOUL FOR A KLONDIKE BAR.

You can always tell if a woman has met Chuck Norris because the words "Chuck Norris Approved" fade with the bruises.

Not to be outdone by *Steven Seagal: Lawman*, Chuck Norris is currently producing a new reality series entitled *Chuck Norris Will Bang Your Sister*.

THE LYRICS TO "LOVEGAME" ARE TAKEN FROM A VALENTINE'S DAY CARD SENT FROM LADY GAGA TO CHUCK NORRIS.

Chuck Norris's alarm wakes him up to the sound of a bombing raid over Vietnam.

CHUCK NORRIS RECEIVED TWO PURPLE HEARTS IN THE WAR ON POVERTY.

The first test for hostage negotiators in training is to convince Chuck Norris to vote Democrat. It is an exercise in learning to deal with defeat.

CHUCK NORRIS KNOCKED DOWN HIS NEIGHBOR'S HOUSE JUST TO GET A BETTER VIEW OF THAT NEIGHBOR'S WIFE TOPLESS.

In five hundred years, pure energy will be observable under a very sophisticated microscope. When viewed, you will be able to see millions of Chuck Norrises doing roundhouse kicks nonstop at an incredible rate. When this happens, Chuck will emerge from his grave after a long sleep, stretch his arms, and casually say, "I cannot be created or destroyed."

CHUCK NORRIS MASTURBATES TO PICTURES OF HIMSELF MASTURBATING.

Chuck Norris does not obey the Law of Conservation of Energy, choosing instead to obey the Law of Distribution of Pain.

Chuck Norris's brief career as a professional narcotics investigator ended after internal affairs raised suspicions about the high number of boot prints admitted into evidence at the crime scenes of the cases he closed.

CHUCK NORRIS WAS ASKED TO LEAVE THE RESERVATION AFTER AN UNFORTUNATE INCIDENT IN WHICH HE MISHEARD THE WORD "WAMPUM."

After a grueling fifteen-minute interview, Chuck Norris drove Nancy Grace to suicide in a ten-foot ditch in the Appalachian woodlands, thirty miles from the nearest town.

After hearing that Jesus had fed multitudes with five loaves of bread and two fish, Chuck Norris fed the entire population of India with just the crumbs in his mustache.

If you put a picture of Chuck Norris on a record and play it backward, you'll hear the *Walker, Texas Ranger* theme song followed by a raspy voice that says, "Seven days." Seven days later, Chuck Norris will explode into your home and raid your refrigerator.

Chuck Norris enjoys ruining the endings of Harry Potter books for children. When they start crying, Chuck Norris calmly says, "I'll give you something to cry about," and roundhouse kicks them in the face.

CHUCK NORRIS CAN MAKE COMMUNISM WORK, BUT HE NEVER WOULD.

On a hot Texas day, Chuck Norris heard someone say, "It's not the heat, it's the humidity that will kill you." Chuck immediately threw him into the sun.

Chuck Norris is no longer a noun; it is a verb.

Chuck Norris once had sex on the beach. The lucky woman exploded from the sheer force of his ejaculation. However, his sperm lived on and occasionally wash up on shore, where they are mistakenly identified as giant squid.

CHUCK NORRIS DOESN'T GET MORNING WOOD, HE GETS MORNING REDWOOD.

Chuck Norris destroyed Rainforest Cafe to launch an international logging operation.

CHUCK NORRIS CAN INFLATE A BALLOON WITH ONE FART.

In the interest of public safety, the state of Oregon banned the sale of Volkswagens after Chuck Norris learned the "punch buggy" game.

At this very moment, there is a fifty-fifty chance that **CHUCK NORRIS IS BONING YOUR SISTER.**

CHUCK NORRIS IS THE REASON WHY YOU TOUCH YOURSELF AT NIGHT.

The Experience Music Project in Seattle was closed for three weeks after Chuck Norris's visit when he wanted to experience oral sex with a life-size wax statue of Susan Boyle.

Chuck Norris's TiVo records only John Wayne movies, old Ronald Reagan speeches, and *Walker, Texas Ranger.*

CHUCK NORRIS HAS NEVER USED A QUESTION MARK IN HIS ENTIRE LIFE.

In his will, Chuck Norris demands that he must perform his own autopsy.

Chuck Norris once abandoned one of his sons when it was discovered he was allergic to the family dog.

EVEN SWITZERLAND SUPPORTS CHUCK NORRIS.

Chuck Norris's ringtone is the sound of the space shuttle taking off during an air raid drill.

CHUCK NORRIS'S SPERM IS SO VIRILE THAT IT TRAVELED BACK IN TIME AND IMPREGNATED HIS MOTHER. ONLY CHUCK NORRIS COULD FATHER CHUCK NORRIS.

The only word in the English language that rhymes with "orange" is "Chuck Norris."

CHUCK NORRIS USES HIS PENIS TO LOOK AROUND CORNERS.

Chuck Norris knows an astounding magic trick where he asks you to pick a card and then punches you in the solar plexus.

CHUCK NORRIS KNOWS VICTORIA'S SECRET.

Chuck Norris conducts all official business on the roof of a train speeding toward a low-clearance tunnel.

CHUCK NORRIS DOESN'T WAIT FOR OPPORTUNITY TO COME KNOCKING. HE ROUNDHOUSE KICKS IT TILL HE GETS WHAT HE WANTS.

A Kevlar bathing suit is required attire if Chuck Norris ever invites you over to "shoot some pool."

Beethoven's Symphony no. 9 in D Minor was composed after he read a story about a bearded commando in the jungles of Vietnam.

CHUCK NORRIS MUST REAPPLY EVERY FIVE YEARS TO RENEW HIS LICENSE TO MESS WITH TEXAS.

The Zamboni was named after Chuck Norris.

Chuck Norris doesn't bathe like the rest of us. The only baths Chuck Norris takes are bloodbaths.

When Chuck Norris says, "Fuck you and the horse you rode in on," he's announcing his intentions.

CHUCK NORRIS DOESN'T KNOW THE MEANING OF WARTIME—ALL HE KNOWS IS GAME TIME.

When people are dying, they are told not to go to the light, because Chuck Norris is there waiting to kill them.

BIGFOOT IS A PIECE OF CHUCK NORRIS'S BEARD THAT GAINED SENTIENCE AND ESCAPED.

If Chuck Norris asks you for a Shirley Temple, he will be expecting a children's musical on DVD, a handle of Maker's Mark, and an ambassadorship to Ghana in twenty-five years.

The next *Mission: Impossible* is rumored to be about Tom Cruise trying to convert Chuck Norris to Scientology.

At their wedding, Chuck Norris and his wife wrote their own vows. She promised to love, honor, and cherish him. He vowed to bring a world of pain to Jim Wertman of Groton, Connecticut. Chuck Norris is a man of his vows.

THE ONLY THING CONGRESS CAN AGREE ABOUT ON HEALTH CARE IS RECOGNIZING CHUCK NORRIS AS THE ONLY LEGAL FORM OF EUTHANASIA.

The lunar lander that brought Neil Armstrong and Buzz Aldrin to the moon was actually a discarded Total Gym prototype.

CHUCK NORRIS SUPPORTS THE PUBLIC OPTION. HE HAS THE OPTION TO PUBLICLY EXECUTE ANYONE HE CHOOSES.

Chuck Norris used to believe in global warming, but only because he was mishearing it as "global warning." Chuck Norris believes the earth deserves a warning before he destroys it.

CHUCK NORRIS SPELLS THE WORD "TEAM" WITH FIVE I'S AND THE CHEROKEE WORD FOR SELF-RELIANCE.

The sight of raisins angers Chuck Norris because he knows they could have been made into Mad Dog 20/20.

SINCE 1984, ALL OF KEITH RICHARDS'S BLOOD HAS BEEN PROVIDED BY CHUCK NORRIS.

Chuck Norris never thinks twice because three times is just too many.

In response to his challenge, Chuck Norris roundhouse kicked MC Hammer so hard that he went bankrupt. Chuck Norris then bellowed, "I can touch this," while he thrusted his pelvis in Hammer's direction.

TO CHUCK NORRIS, DOORKNOBS AND TOILETS ARE SEEN AS MERELY SUGGESTIONS.

Over a dozen traveling salesmen have died of starvation walking up Chuck Norris's driveway.

CHUCK NORRIS CIRCUMCISED HIMSELF. AT BIRTH. WITH HIS BARE HANDS.

Chuck Norris CAN find a needle in a haystack, and then kill a man with the needle . . . or the haystack.

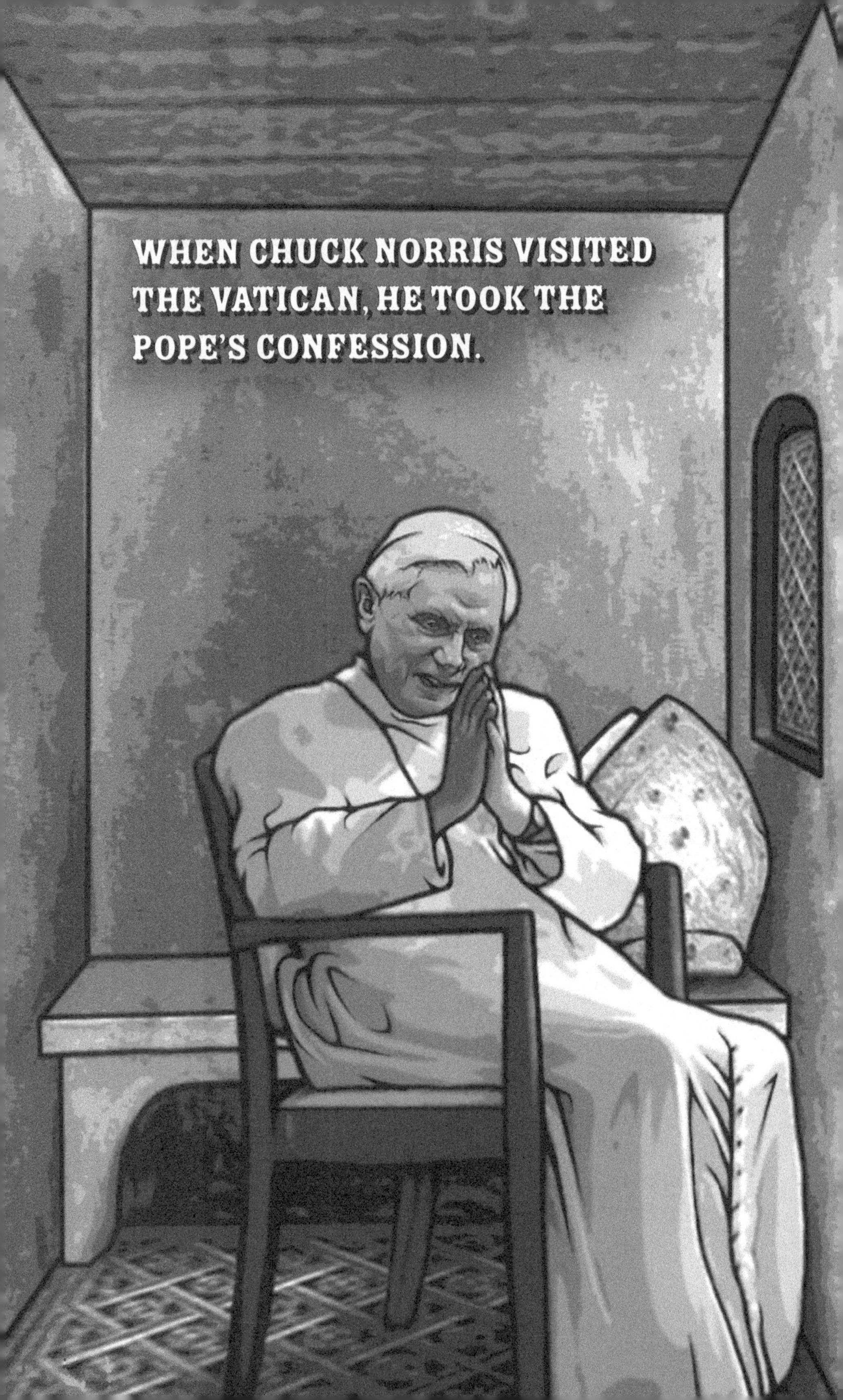
WHEN CHUCK NORRIS VISITED
THE VATICAN, HE TOOK THE
POPE'S CONFESSION.

Chuck Norris constructed his own iPod by staring intensely at ten thousand country-western bands until they fearfully compacted themselves into a 2 x 4 x ½ – inch white rectangle.

CHUCK NORRIS INVENTED HEAVY METAL MUSIC AFTER LED ZEPPELIN ASKED HIM TO BUILD A GUITAR OUT OF A SOLID BLOCK OF IRON.

Chuck Norris stopped telling jokes when he got tired of people laughing out of nervousness.

President Nixon was forced to resign when he learned Chuck Norris considered him "too goddamn liberal."

Chuck Norris likes his coffee the way he likes his justice: **INSTANT.**

CHUCK NORRIS IS SO COOL THAT THE POPE HAS A FISH DECAL ON HIS CAR WITH THE WORD "NORRIS" INSIDE.

Chuck Norris's shoes, most notably the one that roundhouse kicked down the Berlin Wall, are kept in a secret government closet in Langley, Virginia.

CHUCK NORRIS TELLS TIME BY STARING DIRECTLY INTO THE SUN.

Chuck Norris never wet his bed as a child. The bed wet itself out of fear.

Chuck Norris combs his beard with a brush made of Na'vi hair.

Chuck Norris's jock strap was once nominated for best actor in a supporting role.

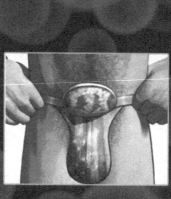

ACADEMY
AWARDS

Chuck Norris was banned from *Fox and Friends* after his beard was found making out with Geraldo Rivera's mustache in the greenroom.

CHUCK NORRIS'S BODY ODOR SMELLS LIKE TEEN SPIRIT.

Chuck Norris can play a perfect rendition of Gustav Holst's The Planets on a comb covered with a Kleenex.

Chuck Norris's backyard barbecue grill is used to cook every hot dog sold at Houston Astros home games.

Chuck Norris went into a kindergarten to talk about fire safety. After four minutes, three children were on fire and Chuck had shot a bottle-rocket out of his urethra.

CHUCK NORRIS PERFORMS COLD FUSION IN HIS LEFT TESTICLE, AND NUCLEAR FISSION IN HIS RIGHT.

Chuck Norris was cast as the protagonist in *The Terminator*, but he later bowed out of the role, since he has already stopped a time war between machines and mankind. Twice.

CHUCK NORRIS: IMPREGNATING VIRGINS, AND KEEPING THEM THAT WAY, SINCE 9 MONTHS B.C.

Chuck Norris actually sang the *Walker, Texas Ranger* theme song. This is not a joke. He actually fucking sang it.

Chuck Norris's nipples are a lot like the great pyramids: They're hard as stone, four hundred feet tall, and worshiped by the ancient Egyptians.

CHUCK NORRIS PUTS OUT
FOREST FIRES BY TAKING A PISS.

Chuck Norris bought the land for his ranch from
Donald Trump for a handful of beads.

Much to the chagrin of all the single ladies, Chuck
Norris likes it but he'll never put a ring on it. However,
he will put a ring around your eye.

CHUCK NORRIS CAN
DEEP-THROAT A WIFFLEBALL BAT.

Chuck Norris can grant wishes, as long as you wish for
roundhouse kicks to the face or a Total Gym.

FOR EVERY MAN YOU DON'T KILL, CHUCK NORRIS KILLS SEVEN.

When people say, "God Bless America," they're really saying, "God Bless Chuck Norris," because due to a 1952 decree by Congress, the terms "Chuck Norris" and "America" are interchangeable.

DEBBIE DID DALLAS BECAUSE SHE COULDN'T HANDLE CHUCK NORRIS.

World War I was started after Chuck Norris decided there were too many goddamn people in Europe.

Chuck Norris once passed a kidney stone in the shape and size of William Shatner, which sold at auction for $7 million.

The long lines at airports are caused by auctions of autographed Chuck Norris body scans.

EVERY FOUR YEARS, CHUCK NORRIS BEATS ANOTHER TWENTY-FOUR HOURS INTO FEBRUARY.

When an airport worker told Chuck Norris that his flight was delayed, he told her that her pregnancy was delayed and did jumping jacks on her uterus.

GOD WANTED TEN DAYS TO CREATE THE WORLD. CHUCK NORRIS GAVE HIM SIX.

IF CHUCK NORRIS WERE AN ANIMAL, HE WOULD BE A CHUCK NORRIS.

Chuck Norris burned his eyeballs out with cigarettes just to prove to some eighth-grade students that smoking is dangerous.

CHUCK NORRIS'S FAVORITE SMELL IS THAT OF HIS OPPONENT'S SOILED PANTS.

If you want to wear the same cologne as Chuck Norris, you'll be disappointed to find that Chuck Norris doesn't wear cologne. For two hundred dollars, however, Mr. Norris will fart on your chest before you go on a date.

CHUCK NORRIS HAS A GUESTHOUSE MADE ENTIRELY OUT OF JOAN RIVERS'S VAGINA.

The great Chicago fire of 1871 was not, in fact, started by Mrs. O'Leary's cow. The fire was started by Chuck Norris when he discovered that deep-dish pizza had not yet been invented.

Someone once put Chuck Norris on hold. That's where the term "choke hold" comes from.

THE ENERGIZER BUNNY IS ACTUALLY
CHUCK NORRIS IN A RABBIT SUIT.

DAFT PUNK'S "HARDER, BETTER, FASTER, STRONGER" WAS ORIGINALLY TITLED "CHUCK NORRIS."

GOD WONDERS IF CHUCK NORRIS IS HUMAN, BECAUSE HE SURE AS HELL NEVER CREATED HIM.

There has never been a Hurricane Chuck because that would just be redundant.

CHUCK NORRIS HAS TWO SPEEDS: "KILL" AND "FUCK YOUR GIRLFRIEND."

Two and a Half Men was originally a show only about Chuck Norris.

If international politics were a nail, Chuck Norris would be the hammer. If international politics were a chance for all men to embrace each other and live in peace, Chuck Norris would be the hammer.

If MacGyver and Chuck were locked in a room together, Chuck would make a bomb out of MacGyver and get out.

CHUCK NORRIS IS THE FOUNDER OF ALL MODERN PSYCHOANALYSIS.

Not only does Chuck Norris talk in the third person, he sees in the third person.

CHUCK NORRIS TAKES NO PRISONERS, BUT HE DOES TAKE THEIR WIVES.

Life is like a box of chocolates. You never know when Chuck Norris is going to kill you.

SEISMOLOGY IS THE STUDY OF CHUCK NORRIS'S MASTURBATION HABITS.

Chuck Norris successfully mated a graham cracker with a knife.

On Chuck Norris's doghouse there is a sticker that says **BEWARE OF CHUCK NORRIS.**

CHUCK NORRIS IS THE ONLY PERSON KANYE WEST WON'T INTERRUPT.

Chuck Norris is a lot like fine wine: He only gets better with age; and if you hang around with him long enough, you'll probably wake up in a daze, with no money and a boot mark imprinted in your skull.

Chuck Norris is a philanthropist. He donated his chest hair to make the noose that hung Saddam Hussein.

No man is an island, and neither is Chuck Norris. He's what you call a continent.

A SOLAR ECLIPSE IS THE SUN'S ATTEMPT TO HIDE FROM CHUCK NORRIS.

Chuck Norris roundhouse kicked his grandmother in the mouth on Christmas morning. Socks again.

WHEN THE GOING GETS TOUGH, THE GOING IS CHANNELING CHUCK NORRIS.

Chuck Norris played the tornado in the movie *Twister*.

When you ask Chuck Norris for an autograph, he burns his name onto your soul with his eye lasers.

Chuck Norris doesn't lie. He bends the truth with his massive biceps.

CHUCK NORRIS DOES NOT RECOGNIZE ALBANY AS THE CAPITAL OF NEW YORK.

Matthew Webb was the first person to swim the English Channel. Chuck Norris was the first person to swim the Sea of Tranquility.

BLITZKRIEG IS THE GERMAN WORD FOR CHUCK NORRIS.

The phrase **MADE BY CHUCK NORRIS** is imprinted beneath the surface of China.

EVERY TIME CHUCK NORRIS KILLS SOMEONE, AN ANGEL GETS ITS BEARD.

When Chuck Norris talks about "pumping iron," he's actually referring to masturbation.

Chuck Norris has 189 STDs, including six found only in sharks.

CHUCK NORRIS IS ALLOWED TO TALK ABOUT FIGHT CLUB.

The term "TGIF" was coined when statisticians found that Friday is the day with the lowest number of deaths caused by Chuck Norris.

WHEN GOD SNEEZES, THE SERAPHIM SING, "CHUCK BLESS YOU."

Since the presence of Chuck Norris drives women wild with desire and makes men quake with terror, it is very disruptive to film him with other actors. For each episode of *Walker, Texas Ranger*, Chuck Norris filmed his scenes in front of a blue screen and the other actors were digitally added later. This is why his acting appears, occasionally, to be a little wooden.

WHEN CHUCK NORRIS MAKES LOVE, IT'S LIKE WAR.

WHEN OBAMA SAID, "YES, WE CAN," HE REALLY MEANT "YES, WE CAN, AS LONG AS CHUCK NORRIS SAYS IT'S ALL RIGHT."

Katy Perry kissed a girl because Chuck Norris told her to. She didn't have a choice but to like it.

CHUCK NORRIS MAKES THE WORLD GO 'ROUND. HE LITERALLY SPINS IT WITH HIS INDEX FINGER.

A full-scale replica of Chuck Norris's penis was erected in Toronto. It was named the CN Tower in his honor.

**Chuck Norris can kill
two stones with one bird.**

Chuck Norris allows churches to exist only in order to stop people from coming and praying at his house.

CHUCK NORRIS WAS THE FIRST BLACK PRESIDENT.

On orders from Chuck Norris, Crayola created a Chuck Norris–colored crayon. No matter what you try to draw, a picture of Chuck giving you a thumbs-up appears.

Chuck Norris used to date Helen Keller, but when he whispered sweet nothings into her ears she went deaf, and when he showed her his wang she went blind.

Chuck Norris's simple trick to getting ketchup out of a glass bottle is to travel back in time and prevent the invention of ketchup by assassinating H. J. Heinz with a blow dart.

Chuck Norris once tried to masturbate, but it quickly devolved into an arm wrestling match between his penis and his palm.

Physicists had long noted certain anomalies in their readings, which spiked every July fourth. Decades of research and millions and dollars confirmed their hypothesis that Chuck Norris's patriotism-induced boner was so powerful that it was warping the fabric of space-time.

CHUCK NORRIS HAS TO SORT HIS LAUNDRY INTO THREE LOADS: DARKS, WHITES, AND BLOODSTAINS.

An average adult's intestines produce about half a liter of flatulent gas per day. Chuck Norris's intestines produce four feature-length films every year, all written and directed by his spleen.

Chuck Norris can pause live TV without using TiVo. He just tells it to hold still while he gets his roast beef sandwich.

When Google can't find something, **THEY NORRIS IT.**

Chuck Norris once survived a suicide bombing. He was the bomber.

CHUCK NORRIS WAS DISQUALIFIED FROM THE 1992 OLYMPIC SHOT-PUT CHAMPIONSHIP FOR REVERSING THE POLARITY OF EARTH.

Chuck Norris once beat Tiger Woods in golf so bad that Tiger was found at 2:30 A.M. dazed and bloody in a wrecked SUV with no recollection of what had happened.

Chuck Norris's beard has the texture of Go-Gurt when he's happy and barbed wire when he's angry.

THE MCRIB SANDWICH COMES BACK ONLY WHEN CHUCK NORRIS IS IN THE MOOD FOR ONE.

When Chuck Norris helps you jumpstart your car, remember: Beard is positive, fist is negative.

WHILE EVERYONE MADE PAPER AIRPLANES AS A CHILD, CHUCK NORRIS MADE PAPER BEARDS.

The Chuck Norris action figure is responsible for 84 percent of all cases of Sudden Infant Death Syndrome.

On the series finale of *Fear Factor*, Chuck Norris ate Joe Rogan.

A MAN ONCE SPENT THREE DAYS CLIMBING A MOUNTAIN ONLY TO DISCOVER THAT HE WAS SCALING CHUCK NORRIS'S PENIS.

Chuck Norris owns a magical mirror that allows him to peer out of any other mirror in the world. Anytime you undress in front of the mirror in your bedroom, Chuck Norris could be watching. But he never is, because your flabby body disgusts him.

BEFORE CHUCK NORRIS WAS BORN, PEOPLE CRIED ONLY OUT OF HAPPINESS.

Chuck Norris can impregnate a woman in forty-seven ways not involving his penis.

Chuck Norris once spent a night in a hotel in West Virginia. The next day the state promptly changed its name to West Ia.

CHUCK NORRIS WON A CAR ON *THE PRICE IS RIGHT* BY GUESSING THAT A CAN OF TUNA WAS WORTH $9,534.

Chuck Norris and the Dalai Lama combined to become the perfect human being and the Dalai Lama.

Chuck Norris will make you an offer you can't refuse, and then make you refuse it.

THE MOVIE *ANACONDA* WAS FILMED IN CHUCK NORRIS'S PANTS.

The book *How to Eat Fried Worms* was a highly edited version of Chuck Norris's original *How to Decapitate Foreign Delegations.*

CHUCK NORRIS CAN PEEL POTATOES WITH HIS EYELIDS.

Chuck Norris's weakness is that he can't kick ass without eating breakfast. Ironically, he eats ass for breakfast.

The reason newborn babies cry is because they know they have just entered a world with Chuck Norris.

GOD RECENTLY CONVERTED TO CHUCKTIANITY.

If you spell Chuck Norris wrong on Google it doesn't say, "Did you mean: Chuck Norris?" It simply replies, "Run while you still have the chance."

CHUCK NORRIS NEVER RETREATS. HE JUST ATTACKS IN THE OPPOSITE DIRECTION.

If you play Led Zeppelin's "Stairway to Heaven" backward, you'll hear Chuck Norris banging your sister.

CHUCK NORRIS CAN PLAY THE VIOLIN WITH A PIANO.

The hood ornament on Chuck Norris's pickup truck is a live eagle's head.

CHUCK NORRIS'S STAR ON THE HOLLYWOOD WALK OF FAME WAS THE FIRST TO GO SUPERNOVA.

Chuck Norris is a proud sponsor of cement.

CHUCK NORRIS DEFEATED THE CYCLOPS BY PUNCHING HIM BETWEEN THE EYE.

CHUCK NORRIS TURNED GOD INTO AN ATHEIST.

Chuck Norris smokes after sex. Not cigarettes—his penis literally smokes.

CHUCK NORRIS CAN SUCK A FISH COMPLETELY DRY IN ONE BREATH.

Every time Chuck Norris hears the name "Virgin Mary," he chuckles to himself.

Chuck Norris consults a physician when he has an erection lasting less than four hours.

When Chuck Norris was born, the nurse said, "Holy crap! That's Chuck Norris!" Then she had had sex with him. At that point, she was the third woman he had slept with.

CHUCK NORRIS PUTS THE RAGE IN COURAGE.

Vanessa Carlton's hit song "A Thousand Miles" was inspired by the distance Chuck Norris kicked her boyfriend after he stepped on Chuck's snakeskin boots.

A waitress at a Sizzler accidentally gave Chuck Norris a well-done steak instead of a rare steak. Chuck proceeded to have sex with her on the table and said, "Now that's well done!" The waitress replied, "That's pretty rare, too!" Chuck then had sex with her fifteen more times just to prove her wrong.

The opening scene of the movie *Saving Private Ryan* is loosely based on games of dodgeball Chuck Norris played in second grade.

Teenage Mutant Ninja Turtles is based on a true story: Chuck Norris once swallowed a turtle whole, and when he crapped it out the turtle was six feet tall and had learned karate.

WHEN YOU'RE CHUCK NORRIS, ANYTHING PLUS ANYTHING IS EQUAL TO ONE. ONE ROUNDHOUSE KICK TO THE FACE.

Chuck Norris never goes to the dentist, because his teeth are unbreakable. His enemies never go to the dentist, because they have no teeth.

CHUCK NORRIS ONCE PULLED OUT A SINGLE HAIR FROM HIS BEARD AND SKEWERED THREE MEN THROUGH THE HEART WITH IT.

IF YOU WORK IN AN OFFICE WITH CHUCK NORRIS, DON'T ASK HIM FOR HIS THREE-HOLE PUNCH.

In the beginning there was nothing. And then Chuck Norris roundhouse kicked that nothing in the face and said, "Get a job." That is the story of the universe.

Coroners refer to dead people as "ABC"s: Already Been Chucked.

What was going through the minds of all of
Chuck Norris's victims before they died? His shoe.

CHUCK NORRIS DOESN'T HAVE A COMPUTER. JUST A BASEMENT FULL OF ASIAN KIDS WHO MEMORIZE NUMBERS.

If you are within one mile of Chuck Norris and you
drop your toast, it will always land butter-side up.
Always.

Chuck Norris doesn't believe in rubber condoms.
Instead, he sticks his penis in a girl, and uses that girl
as a condom while fucking another.

CHUCK NORRIS CAN PLAY A BITCHIN' EARDRUM SOLO.

The French did not send the Statue of Liberty to the United States as a sign of peace. They were trying to win a bet that Chuck Norris couldn't fuck a one-hundred-fifty-foot-tall copper woman. Boy, were they wrong.

Chuck Norris has the heart of a child. **HE KEEPS IT IN A SMALL BOX.**

Chuck Norris invented the Spanish language because he liked the word "*pantalones*" and needed a language to use it in context.

When Chuck Norris gets pulled over, he lets the cop off with a warning.

CHUCK NORRIS PLAYS BATTLESHIP WITH THE U.S. NAVY.

ALL of Chuck Norris's genes are dominant.

WHEN CHUCK NORRIS
TELLS TIME, TIME OBEYS.

Chuck Norris can tell which way a train traveled by looking at the tracks.

Chuck Norris GENOCIDER is the official drink of the United Nations.

CHUCK NORRIS BUILT
THE HOSPITAL HE WAS BORN IN.

The original name for the popular video game *Halo* was *Chuck Norris Superkicks II: Alien Fuck-Up Hour.*

If Chuck Norris makes a woman ride on top during sex, she instantly qualifies for the Mile High Club.

ASTRONAUTS DREAM OF BECOMING CHUCK NORRIS WHEN THEY GROW UP.

The truth will set you free. Chuck Norris will set you on fire.

Chuck Norris can tie someone's hands behind their back with his hands tied behind his back.

CHUCK NORRIS COMPOSED THE SOUNDTRACK TO "2 GIRLS 1 CUP."

CELEBRITIES DIE IN THREES BECAUSE
FOR CHUCK NORRIS, KILLING JUST ONE
CELEBRITY IS NEVER ENOUGH.

Jaws made his last cinematic appearance in 1987. Coincidentally, Chuck Norris developed a liking for sushi in 1987.

LIFE COMES AT YOU FAST. CHUCK NORRIS'S FIST COMES AT YOU FASTER.

Some people see the glass half full, others see the glass as half empty. Chuck Norris always sees Scotch.

AS A POOR COLLEGE STUDENT, CHUCK NORRIS WENT TO THE LOCAL SPERM BANK TO MAKE SOME QUICK CASH. HE RETIRED LATER THAT DAY.

Chuck Norris is just like Spider-Man, only instead of being bitten by a radioactive spider, Chuck was bitten by a radioactive god.

CHUCK NORRIS CAN PLAY RUSSIAN ROULETTE WITH A FULLY LOADED REVOLVER AND WIN.

All eleven secret herbs and spices used in KFC can be found naturally in Chuck Norris's beard.

CHUCK NORRIS ONCE GOT A GIRL PREGNANT AFTER PHONE SEX.

People don't actually die of "natural causes." It's just a phrase doctors use because there are only so many times you can say "Chuck Norris did it again" in one day.

THE FRENCH SURRENDER TO CHUCK NORRIS EVERY DAY AT 2 P.M.

GIRAFFES WERE CREATED AFTER CHUCK NORRIS UPPERCUTTED A HORSE.

Leading hand sanitizers claim they can kill 99.9 percent of germs. Chuck Norris can kill 100 percent of whatever the fuck he wants.

SOME KIDS PISS THEIR NAME IN THE SNOW. CHUCK NORRIS CAN PISS HIS NAME INTO CONCRETE.

The Burning Man festival got its start when Chuck Norris set fire to a bunch of hippies with his eyebeams.

Every time Chuck Norris throws a penny in a fountain, there is a 0.017 percent increase in the value of the Canadian dollar.

WITH AN ACCURATE KICK TO THE NECK, CHUCK NORRIS CAN TURN ANY FRUIT INTO A VEGETABLE.

Danny Bonaduce will be playing the role of Chuck Norris in the autobiographical musical of his life, *Badass in Denim.*

The one time Chuck Norris says that he blacked out, he woke up to a room where women were naked, necks were broken, and a goat was wearing a T-shirt that read **TEAM DELTA FORCE**.

Chuck Norris once defeated a steam train in a jousting tournament.

CHUCK NORRIS DOESN'T CHEAT DEATH. HE WINS FAIR AND SQUARE.

Toward the end of Super Bowl XLIV, Chuck Norris placed a friendly $1 bet on the New Orleans Saints.

Chuck Norris eats the core of an apple first.

Chuck Norris once chopped down a cherry tree with his dick. When George Washington's father asked him who chopped down the cherry tree, Chuck Norris responded by banging George Washington's mom. It is for this reason that Chuck Norris is known as "the Grandfather of Our Country."

CHUCK NORRIS ONCE WON A GAME OF CONNECT FOUR IN THREE MOVES.

Chuck Norris doesn't have hair on his testicles because hair does not grow on steel.

The best part of waking up is not Folgers in your cup, but knowing that Chuck Norris didn't kill you in your sleep.

CHAMPIONS ARE THE BREAKFAST OF CHUCK NORRIS.

CHUCK NORRIS JIZZES LIGHTNING BOLTS.

Chuck Norris became one-fourth Cherokee after winning the 1999 "Who Can Eat a Jeep?" competition.

BEFORE AIRBUS MADE PLANES,
THEY MANUFACTURED CITY BUSSES FOR
CHUCK NORRIS TO PLAY CATCH WITH.

JACK WAS NIMBLE, JACK WAS QUICK, BUT JACK STILL COULDN'T DODGE CHUCK NORRIS'S ROUNDHOUSE KICK.

When God said, "Let there be light," Chuck Norris replied, "Say please."

THERE'S STRONG. THEN THERE'S ARMY STRONG. THEN THERE'S CHUCK NORRIS STRONG.

Most men are okay with their wives fantasizing about Chuck Norris during sex because they are doing the same thing.

If at first you don't succeed, **YOU OBVIOUSLY AREN'T CHUCK NORRIS.**

The city of Dallas was brought to a stand still after they renamed their main thoroughfare Chuck Norris Boulevard. Residents were terrified to cross Chuck Norris.

CHUCK NORRIS CAN WATCH A SEASON OF *24* IN JUST THREE HOURS.

Chuck Norris's family wraps his gifts in lead so he can't see what's inside.

If a tree falls in the forest and nobody is around to hear it, not only does Chuck Norris hear it, he probably had something to do with it.

Chuck Norris can set ants on fire with a magnifying glass—at night.

CHUCK NORRIS CAN TIE HIS SHOES WITH HIS FEET.

When international spies are given a "license to kill,"
they are simply handed a picture of Chuck Norris.

THE FIRST RUNNING OF THE BULLS TOOK PLACE WHEN CHUCK NORRIS VISITED PAMPLONA TO SEE THE TOWN'S PRIZED LIVESTOCK.

Chuck Norris keeps a revolver, two plane tickets
to Brazil, and a year's supply of emergency
contraceptives in his toolbox.

THE WORLD WAS ACTUALLY FLAT UNTIL CHUCK NORRIS MADE IT CURL UP IN A BALL OF FEAR.

My wife and I decided to name our son Chuck Norris. My
wife is still in a coma, and I am learning to walk again.

MEAT LOAF WOULD DO ANYTHING FOR CHUCK NORRIS.

The only thing that gets between Chuck Norris and justice is an equal sign.

When dining out, Chuck Norris writes thoughtful and practical advice in the area on the bill marked "Tip."

CHUCK NORRIS HAS BEEN TO MARS. THAT'S WHY THERE'S NO LIFE THERE.

In his will, Chuck Norris has specified that *if* he dies, he will bury himself.

CHUCK NORRIS BUILT A TIME MACHINE SIMPLY SO HE COULD REWATCH *BACK TO THE FUTURE* DURING ITS ORIGINAL THEATRICAL RUN.

To raise their standards of safety, automakers now crash test their cars by paying Chuck Norris to run into them.

CHUCK NORRIS TAKES STEROIDS, BUT ONLY SO THAT HIS BALLS WILL FIT IN HIS PANTS.

The Large Hadron Collider hasn't discovered anything new yet because Chuck Norris is still using it to warm up some Hot Pockets.

In an effort to stop teens from smoking, the Surgeon General's warning on cigarettes will soon be replaced with an illustration of a glaring Chuck Norris.

CHUCK NORRIS DOES NOT HAVE A SEAT ON THE U.N. SECURITY COUNCIL; HE HAS A COUCH.

Chuck Norris's orgasm is the number one cause of drowning among women between the ages of eighteen and thirty-five.

Chuck Norris had to give up drinking when gas went over three dollars a gallon.

CHUCK NORRIS CAN BREAK-DANCE ON THIN ICE.

The Mars scenes in *Total Recall* were filmed entirely on Chuck Norris's taint.

Chuck Norris was offered a part on the TV show *Heroes*, but he left after he found out it wasn't a documentary.

Chuck Norris's Rice Krispies don't say shit until he gives them the OK.

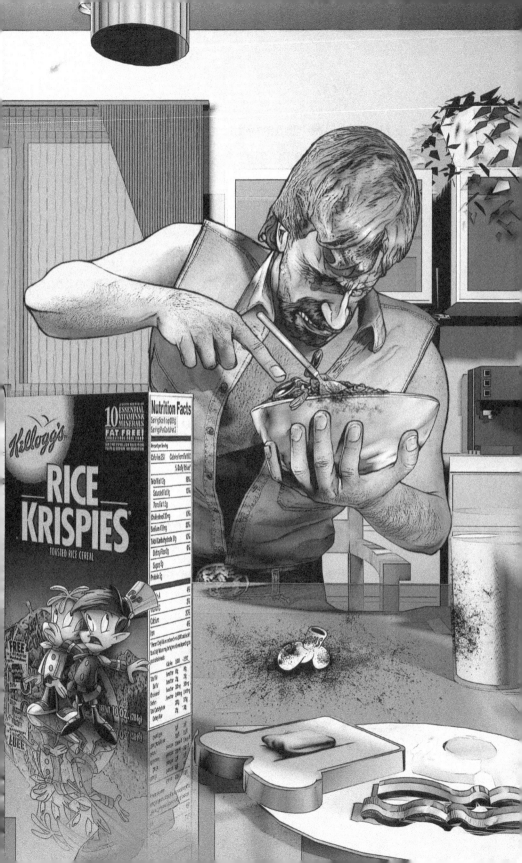

Chuck Norris once defeated four Chinese acrobats in a game of Twister using only his penis.

When Chuck Norris drinks, he never throws up. **HE ONLY THROWS DOWN.**

CHUCK NORRIS CAN CREATE ENOUGH WIND POWER WITH ONE ROUNDHOUSE KICK TO POWER SRI LANKA FOR FORTY DAYS.

Chuck Norris's roundhouse kick is an optical illusion. His right foot doesn't swing around and hit your head, his left foot spins the earth so that your head hits his foot.

CHUCK NORRIS STILL DOESN'T KNOW THAT *WALKER, TEXAS RANGER* IS JUST A TV SHOW.

For six years, Chuck Norris was the FBI's chief negotiator. His job involved calling up criminals and saying, "This is Chuck Norris."

WHEN CHUCK NORRIS WANTS POPCORN, HE EXHALES ON NEBRASKA.

CHUCK NORRIS'S COMPUTER HAS A LIVE MOUSE ATTACHED TO IT.

Chuck Norris can do a handstand with both hands tied behind his back.

After the deaths of ten child actors, the producers of *Sidekicks* finally decided to cut the scene where Chuck Norris pats the kid on the back for winning the tournament.

CHUCK NORRIS ONCE PULLED A BUILDING OUT OF A BURNING BUILDING.

When a reporter asked Chuck about his decision to shave his beard, Chuck replied, "If I told you, I'd have to kill you." He then laughed a little bit, realizing that he was going to kill the reporter anyway.

IN BASEBALL, A PLAYER IS SAID TO HAVE EXECUTED A CHUCK NORRIS WHEN HE SCORES TEN OR MORE RUNS IN A SINGLE AT BAT.

Chuck Norris owns a custom belt sander with three settings: Low, High, and Shave.

Chuck Norris once hit the lottery. It was pronounced dead at the scene.

Fire escapes were invented to protect fire from Chuck Norris.

"HIGH TIDE" AND "LOW TIDE" ACTUALLY REFER TO THE TIMES WHEN CHUCK NORRIS GETS IN AND OUT OF THE OCEAN.

Chuck Norris went to the DMV and the clerk asked him for three forms of ID. He gave her a roundhouse kick, a whisker from his beard, and a *Walker, Texas Ranger* DVD.

A woman who once gave Chuck Norris a blow job died of tetanus.

CHUCK NORRIS'S MORNING RUN IS ALONG THE AUTOBAHN.

On his birthday, Chuck Norris randomly selects one lucky child to be thrown into the sun.

Chuck Norris doesn't have a CTRL key on his keyboard because Chuck Norris is always in control.

CHUCK NORRIS DESCRIBES HIS POLITICS AS "SOMEWHERE TO THE RIGHT OF HITLER."

Chuck Norris was once charged with three counts of attempted murder in Colorado, but the charges were dropped because Chuck Norris does not "attempt" murder.

Consumer Reports, in their 2010 ranking of toilet papers, found Chuck Norris Texas TP to be the least effective brand on the market. It really is true that Chuck Norris won't take shit from anyone.

CHUCK NORRIS IRONS HIS SHIRTS WHILE HE'S STILL WEARING THEM.

Chuck Norris is such a good salesman that he once talked an Amish housewife into buying a plug-in dildo.

Chuck Norris once beat an orphan to death **WITH THE BODY OF ANOTHER ORPHAN.**

Chuck Norris keeps the undefeated 1972 Miami Dolphins in a large tank in his backyard.

CHUCK NORRIS SHOT UP HEROIN FOR ELEVEN MONTHS JUST TO PROVE HOW EASY IT WAS FOR HIM TO QUIT.

CROP CIRCLES ARE CHUCK'S WAY OF TELLING THE WORLD THAT SOMETIMES CORN NEEDS TO LIE THE FUCK DOWN.

A priest, a rabbi, and a minister walk into a bar. Chuck Norris roundhouse kicks them all in the face because he already knows the joke isn't going to be funny enough.

CHUCK NORRIS HAS A CLOSET FULL OF EXPLODING PANTS.

There are only weapons of mass destruction in Iraq when Chuck Norris visits.

ROOSTERS CROW IN THE MORNING TO WARN EVERYONE THAT CHUCK NORRIS IS NOW AWAKE.

While his vision may be compromised at night, Chuck Norris always has perfect death perception.

Chuck Norris puts all his eggs in one basket and then stomps on the basket. Chuck Norris will not spend his time worrying about eggs.

CHUCK NORRIS GOES EASTER EGG HUNTING WITH A LOADED SHOTGUN.

In the movie *Titanic*, Chuck Norris has a brief cameo as "The Iceberg" in hopes of making the movie end sooner.

Chuck Norris invented the speed bump in 1958 when he left several corpses on a residential street and forgot to bury them in his flower garden.

Socrates was put to death after he posed the following philosophical puzzle to Chuck Norris: "Why did you sleep with my wife?"

CHUCK NORRIS CAN MAKE AN ENTIRE BAG OF MICROWAVE POPCORN JUST BY SLIPPING IT DOWN HIS PANTS.

Chuck Norris doesn't have an open-door policy but he does have a closed-fist policy.

WINDOWS VISTA RUNS JUST FINE ON CHUCK NORRIS'S COMPUTER.

Chuck Norris can squeeze apple juice out of a banana.

In 1968 Chuck Norris went on summer holiday to London. He walked into a pub in St. John's Wood and promptly drank a full keg of Guinness. When the bartender asked him to pay his tab, Chuck Norris produced an enormous belch that lasted for ninety-three minutes and thirty-three seconds. Tape recorders running in a nearby recording studio captured this magical event and today we know this recording as the Beatles' *The White Album*.

JESUS COULD WALK ON WATER, BUT CHUCK NORRIS CAN SWIM THROUGH LAND.

Chuck Norris penned "If You're Happy and You Know it, Clap Your Hands" as a way to find victims.

CHUCK NORRIS WON THE 1993 INTERNATIONAL JUMP ROPE CHAMPIONSHIP STANDING COMPLETELY STILL.

A sequel to *300* is currently being filmed starring Chuck Norris. It will be called *1*.

CHUCK NORRIS NEVER USES RUSSIAN DRESSING.

The first dive bar was created when Chuck Norris built a saloon on the floor of Boston Harbor.

Chuck Norris once gave himself a lethal injection of potassium chloride to see if it would give him a buzz.

THE ONLY CROWN CHUCK NORRIS RECOGNIZES IS THE FORD CROWN VICTORIA.

Conan O'Brien once installed a lever next to his desk that, when pulled, played a clip from *Walker, Texas Ranger.* In response, Chuck Norris installed a lever next to his desk that, when pulled, played footage of Chuck Norris having sex with Conan O'Brien's wife.

CHUCK NORRIS'S BARBER USES A BLOWTORCH AND THE JAWS OF LIFE TO TRIM HIS BEARD.

One time a third grader tried to impress Chuck Norris by burping the alphabet. In turn Chuck belched the entire *Gangs of New York* screenplay.

Hulk Hogan cried when he found out that his daughter Brooke had lost her virginity, but was really psyched when he found out that it was to Chuck Norris.

CHUCK NORRIS WAS INVITED TO PLAY A GAME OF CAPTURE THE FLAG AND WON AFTER TAKING OVER ALL OF EUROPE.

Once a year, the National Undertaker's Union holds a party in honor of Chuck Norris.

CHUCK NORRIS IS SO MANLY, HE SNEEZES GUNPOWDER.

Chuck Norris is planning to open up a chain of retail stores called "Bloodbath and Beyond."

MERRIAM-WEBSTER PRINTS A CUSTOM DICTIONARY FOR CHUCK NORRIS THAT DOESN'T HAVE THE WORD "REMORSE" IN IT.

Chuck Norris traced his ancestry back to Chuck Norris.

CHUCK NORRIS WAS THE BEST MAN AT HIS OWN WEDDING.

Chuck Norris shot his age at Pebble Beach when he was seventeen.

UNLIKE SANTA, CHUCK NEVER HAS TO CHECK HIS LIST TWICE.

The fatalities in *Mortal Kombat* are actually re-creations of eyewitness accounts of Chuck Norris going ape shit during a traffic jam.

A monument still stands in memory of the events of October 12, 1983, when Chuck Norris high-fived every single man, woman, and child in Biloxi, Mississippi.

UNSOLVED MYSTERIES WAS REALLY A DOCUMENTARY ABOUT CHUCK NORRIS'S GREATEST ACCOMPLISHMENTS.

Chuck Norris funds his charity for teaching martial arts to underprivileged kids from the proceeds of a professional mixed martial arts fighting league. This is actually true.

CHUCK NORRIS WON THE DAYTONA 500 ON THE BLACK DIRT BIKE FROM *DELTA FORCE*.

CHUCK NORRIS PERSONALLY
BUTCHERED EVERY ANIMAL
FOR LADY GAGA'S MEAT DRESS.

Every year on his birthday, Chuck Norris closes his eyes, wishes his hardest to meet George Bush, Sr., and blows out the candles.

The average human sperm has a 1 in 600 chance of becoming a human. Chuck Norris's sperm has a 1 in 10 chance of being wanted for murder in four states.

WHEN LIFE GIVES CHUCK NORRIS LEMONS, HE MAKES ORANGE JUICE.

The role of Alf, from the hit eighties TV show of the same name, was actually played by Chuck Norris's penis.

THE DIFFERENCE BETWEEN CHUCK NORRIS AND GOD IS THAT CHUCK NORRIS DOES NOT THINK HE'S GOD.

Chuck Norris exists only because he kicked a man so hard that he flew back in time and fell in love with his mother.

Chuck Norris cultivates a small population of third-world orphans with red hair so he can harvest them at a moment's notice for his beard.

Parker Brothers created a special edition of Monopoly just for Chuck Norris. In his set, all of the Community Chest and Chance cards award him first place in a beauty contest.

CHUCK NORRIS'S RAP SHEET ACTUALLY RHYMES.

Whenever Chuck Norris makes a joke, the sound of an audience laughing comes from out of nowhere. Chuck will then turn to you, smile, and give you two thumbs up. After that, everything freezes; even *you* are unable to move. The laughter then turns into music as credits begin to scroll down from thin air. Finally, your sight fades to black and there is nothing. When you regain your vision and mobility, Chuck Norris is nowhere to be found.

ACKNOWLEDGMENTS

Thanks to Kevin Allison, Joe Bianco, Dave Bourla, and Tony Caroselli. A special thanks once more to Angelo Vildasol for his incredible art over the past few years.

ABOUT THE AUTHOR

IAN SPECTOR started the Web phenomenon Chuck Norris Facts back in 2005 and is the *New York Times* bestselling author of *The Truth About Chuck Norris*, *Chuck Norris vs. Mr. T*, and *Chuck Norris Cannot Be Stopped.*

Ian is a graduate of Brown University, where he studied cognitive neuroscience, edited the campus humor magazine, and served as the president of the Brown Entrepreneurship Program. He is currently living in Manhattan running a social technology start-up and is a freelance digital strategy consultant. You can see what he's up to and get in touch at IanJSpector.com or follow @IanJSpector on Twitter.

P.O. 0003342512